The Book of
WELLNESS

The Book of
WELLNESS

A Secular Approach to Spirit, Meaning & Purpose

Donald B. Ardell, Ph.D.

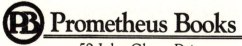

Prometheus Books

59 John Glenn Drive
Amherst, New York 14228-2197

Published 1996 by Prometheus Books

00 99 98 97 96   5 4 3 2 1

Library of Congress Cataloging-in-Publication Data

Ardell, Donald B.
    The book of wellness : a secular approach to spirituality, meaning, & purpose / Donald B. Ardell.
        p.   cm.
    Includes bibliographical references (p.).
    ISBN 1–57392–083–5 (cloth : alk. paper)
    1. Health—Religious aspects. 2. Spiritual life. I. Title.
BL65.M4A73   1996
170'.44—dc20   96–13490
                                                                              CIP

Printed in the United States of America on acid-free paper

Contents

This book is dedicated to
Charles Cochrane
and
John Cleese, Terry Jones, Michael Palin, Eric Idle, and
Everyone Ever Connected with Monty Python's Flying Circus.
Why?
In appreciation for nearly all their work, but particularly for
the movie *The Meaning of Life* and for giving the world this
little insight: "There are many people in this country who,
through no fault of their own, are sane."

Preface

"Visit Our Planetarium, You Tiny, Insignificant Speck in the Universe."

Spotted on a billboard promoting
Boston's Charles Hayden Planetarium.

This book is about ten propositions on meaning and purpose (M&P) in life, starting with my own idea that meaning must be invented time and again as our lives progress. The implications of these propositions for living healthfully and purposefully are explored with the help of some of America's leading wellness experts—one hundred of them, to be exact. However, neither I nor any of the experts wants to convince you to follow his or her meaning of life, but to ponder the possibilities. We all have opinions, theories, and even (in my case) propositions, but some seem more useful than others in terms of health and life satisfaction. While many of these views are likely to be interesting and worth considering, no one is as important as two other views about meaning and purpose (M&P) that this book is designed to explore. Any guesses which two views I'm referring to? Give up?

I'm referring to two views about M&P in life belonging to you!

The first of these views consists of the ideas you currently hold about M&P. You already possess an extraordinarily significant perspective or set of beliefs, impressions, and other leanings about M&P. Your current position on M&P is vital not because it may hold the key to unlocking the secrets of the universe for all men and women, now and forever, but rather because it matters so much to you! This is true even if you hardly ever thought about M&P before now. By reading this book, I think you'll form, with greater clarity than ever before, a conscious picture of precisely *what* you currently think about the meaning and purpose of life. In this fashion, you will become quite consciously aware of what you have decided up to this point in your life, more so than before. For this reason, I suggest that this is one of the two most important views you will come across in this book. This book is a little stage designed to help you clarify things. It has been shaped to make your existing view clearer to you.

Which leads to the second view. This is the biggie, the *Existential King Kong* of M&P, the closest thing you're probably going to get to revelation! (Naturally, this is just a matter of opinion, but you will soon discover I have lots of those—and it's of little or, more likely, no consequence that you agree with any of them.)

Once more, I'll ask if you're with me? Can you sense what I have in mind as to the second view?

I refer to the ideas that you have, or at least decide to pursue, by the time you finish the book! If *The Book of Wellness* does what I wrote it to do, your ideas about M&P will be somewhat different when you're finished reading than they are now.

If I had my way, which I don't seem to get nearly enough for my liking, I might have picked a different title. I might have chosen something like, *The Meaning of Life: 100 Wellness Views, Plus My Own, Plus Your Current View Brought into Sharp Relief, and Finally, a New and Deeper, More Satisfying View by You That Makes the Rest of Us Seem Like Real Dummies, for Nobody Can Decide What M&P Is All about Better Than You Can, after Thinking About It in a Stimulating Fashion.* For some reason, I assumed the publisher wouldn't go for it. Maybe my really accurate and descriptive title didn't have a nice ring to it, or something. Maybe it took up too much space, thus blocking the aisles of bookstores. I don't know. But at least you now understand what I'm trying to do in these pages. Enjoy.

Part One

Introduction

Introduction

"Try to believe in something, but if you believe in nothing, at least do so whole-heartedly."

Ashleigh Brilliant

HEALTH AND THE SEARCH FOR MEANING

This book is about the link between the meaning of life and health status, among other things. That a link exists may seem reasonable to you, but it is not a common perception. To my knowledge, doctors do not ask patients about the meaning of life when hearing symptoms and taking clinical histories. Standard physical exams do not include explorations of existential questions concerning a patient's purposes in life. Well, maybe they should! This and related ideas are explored in these pages.

15

Also explored are the usual age-old philosophical questions but from a wellness view, including, "What's it all about?," "Why are we here?" and "What's the meaning of life?" More than anything else, the focus is on this proposition: A lifelong search for meaning and purpose (M&P) can stimulate, support, and guide you to an exceptionally healthy lifestyle. This is a wellness book focused on a form of spirituality that is not really spiritual at all, at least not spiritual in the usual sense of that word. The phrase "secular spirituality" is an intentional oxymoron, a combination of contradictory or incongruous words. While I am capable of mixing pointedly foolish terms (on occasion truly by accident), in this instance, the deed was a conscious, deliberate act. Even premeditated! I had my reasons, which should become evident as you read on.

The Book of Wellness is not about *the* meaning of life. In my view, it is unlikely that you will ever discover the meaning of life (MOL), since there is no such thing! Even if you did "discover" it, you could later regret having done so, for you might eventually conclude you miscalculated. Let's face it, there are plenty of people on this Earth with absolute answers to the MOL—and all the related questions. They claim to know exactly what all human (and other) life in general and your human life in particular are for—and some of them can be quite insistent that you believe as they do. Make no mistake—taken as a whole, their explanations are creative, varied, and often presented to you with impressive ceremonies and rituals. Unfortunately, their interpretations are rather unsatisfying for many and preposterous to some.

What about you? What do you think? How and why do you believe what you do concerning the meaning of *your* life to date, based on the purposes you have embraced thus far? If you don't have ready answers about which you are confident, don't be concerned. That just might mean that you will derive extra value from this book and find it even more interesting than the millions of others who read it (excuse this bit of positive thinking) who claim to have the MOL all figured out!

EVOLUTION OF AN IDEA

Some people are drawn to a lifelong interest in some form of MOL-related quest for M&P as a consequence of an epiphany of one kind or another. This frequently takes the form of a literal (but more often a figurative) near-death type of experience. Not me. My interest in meaning and purpose grew slowly. When I wrote *High Level Wellness* in 1977, there was no direct mention of the topic of M&P! Of course, I beat around the proverbial bush a bit, but it took another ten years to realize that "spirituality" (a popular term in the health promotion movement), values, and the rest had to be addressed. Eventually, it occurred to me that M&P are more than just relevant— they are keys to the entire wellness concept. Today I believe that these concepts are basic both to the personal pursuit of well-being and to the effective promotion of wellness lifestyles at corporate, institutional, and other levels.

One of the first things I learned in the course of exploring meaning and purpose in a wellness context was that many people in the field are not willing or able to verbalize their positions on what it's all about or what they are doing here on Earth. This surprised me: after all, what could be more consequential? Later, I started to work M&P questions into presentations on the lecture circuit and in graduate courses in health promotion that I've taught at the University of Central Florida in Orlando. Again, most students appeared to be unaccustomed to thinking about these matters, although most were hungry for it once it was exposed in a religion-free context— and they thanked me for doing so afterwards. Over time, I came to the realization that I was on to something.

Eventually, I got the bright idea to conduct a few surveys, first among my fellow triathletes and later among health promotion leaders throughout America (and eventually expanded to Canada and Australia). Rather than attempting such a massive effort on my own, I was assisted by the National Wellness Institute (NWI) of Stevens Point, Wisconsin. The NWI is the preeminent professional organization advancing wellness in the United States, and it annually conducts a conference for wellness promoters attended on average by 1,600 people. It maintains the most complete database on wellness activities, programs, and professionals, and does more to promote the wellness movement than any other organization in America or elsewhere. The NWI made its membership list available to me, encouraged interviews with wellness leaders, and gave me a forum for workshops on M&P at their annual conferences. I did not get very much out of the triathlon community (most are probably too busy training to think very much, at least about their purposes); the wellness network, on the other hand, was a gold mine, once I learned to ask the questions properly! Requesting information regarding the MOL or even how wellness promoters find M&P elicited little response; inviting these folks to respond to the ten propositions discussed throughout this book brought a flood of mail.

Statements were obtained over a three-year period from wellness leaders and practitioners, including physicians, alternative healers, business leaders, fitness experts, and many promoters and practitioners of diverse educational and vocational backgrounds. At first, I accepted only those M&P statements with which I agreed, that is, those I thought were sensible and might be helpful to readers. This meant, of course, I omitted those who provided commentaries I found a bit (or very much) bizarre, such as "the M&P is to worship cows," or "My M&P is to learn to communicate with the Neptunian Telescope People" or "My M&P is to extinguish green people from the face of the Earth." (Yes, there are strange folks in this field, too.) Before long, however, I tempered this bias, after reflecting on the question of "Who am I to decide such a thing?" (I'm the author, that's who!)

Of course, this is not to say that I accepted everything. I decided to use the best one hundred received, with myself (of course) the judge of "best." This choosing task was not so hard at first, but after I reached the five hundred and then the thousand-plus mark, it started to become challenging. There was no way not to be terribly subjective about the matter of selection, so I forgave myself for bias and starting picking favorites, without guilt or remorse. After all, this is *my* book, I reasoned—I'm entitled!

My major criteria in determining the best were that the statements seemed interesting, pleasantly outrageous, somewhat profound, entertaining, or provocative. In addition, I made a decision early on to make this a secular book on meaning and purpose, since I am a secular person. Thus, while I was surprised to receive only a few statements to the effect that "our purpose is to learn to serve and love Almighty God," I made a choice not to use even the few I did obtain. The rationale for this was and remains twofold: (1) there already exists ample support (literary, political, and social) for a theistic explanation of M&P from countless advocates of organized religions; and (2) my personal predispositions run strongly along the secular path. My approach to wellness in general and M&P

in particular favors a rational, nonsupernatural, humanistic orientation to life and its meanings. This rationale will not, of course, please true believers but, doing so has not been a major priority for me in the past so, why should I start now?

In my questionnaires and letters, I asked promoters and practitioners of healthy lifestyles what they thought about the great questions of life (e.g., "What's it all about?" "How do we find M&P?" and so on). The responses picked met my loose preferential criteria—I hope many of them meet yours, as well. Most of all, I hope you find the commentaries and my own materials in the chapters interesting and helpful. On the other hand, I do not care in the least whether you agree with me! Agreement is of no consequence in this matter. What does matter, in my opinion, is discovering that the link between a healthy lifestyle and M&P is exciting, compelling, challenging, and exhilarating.

Eric Hofer, author of *The True Believer,* said if he got one idea from a publication, it was a good read and worth the price. Perhaps you will obtain at least one, maybe lots (one hundred, perhaps) of insights to complement your own quest for M&P from this varied assortment of perspectives. For all the assistance and support provided by the hundred promoters and practitioners of the art and science of wellness as well as the NWI, I am most grateful.

THE WELLNESS CONNECTION

Why do some people live healthy lifestyles while most do not? This question has many answers, spanning the possibilities in both the environmental and biological camps (nature versus nurture). Is there a possibility that your fitness level, the quality of your diet, your sense of humor, your capacity for modifying stress and ability to fashion and sustain a satisfying, healthful lifestyle are all connected to a deeper psychological variable? Specifically, is there a chance that these and other lifestyle matters are affected by how you think, feel, and act concerning just a few of life's great existential questions? I believe this is the case, based on my observations gleaned from more than twenty years as a wellness promoter. I think it's important that we put a bit less energy into promoting fitness, nutrition, and stress management, and a lot more into something a great deal more exciting and profound: exploring meaning in life!

I'm convinced the search for meaning and purpose in life is a crucial success variable in attempts to inform, motivate, and guide ourselves and others to adopt the challenge of living a healthy or wellness lifestyle. In my view, finding challenging meaning and purpose in life ranks as a vital element in the wellness concept.

GETTING A HANDLE ON THE MOL

In a way, the question about M&P could be expressed in broader fashion than basic health. We could ask how it relates to human happiness. All of us, at one time or another, wonder "How can I be happy, or happier?" "What is required for me to have a more satisfying existence, one that makes the most of my resources, talents, life circumstances and so on?" "What are my highest potentials?" Many variations can be conceived. For Mother Teresa-types, M&P seems to be about service to others. On the other hand, for the Jerry Seinfeld types, it might be making people smile, or hoot in merriment, as the case might be! A point to consider is that neither is selfless; both are chosen paths to personal fulfillment or happiness. One wants to be a saint; the other is happiest and most fulfilled when he gets a good laugh. We are not all alike. For a few billion others between and outside these extremes, unique paths to M&P must be found and, I might add, this seems a good thing. A few of us will be noted by history; most will not, despite the rumor of our promised fifteen minutes of fame. Ultimately, our lives are obscure to all but ourselves. What's true for you, as for everyone else, is you must find your own best way to M&P, most of the time with little help along the way. Regrettably, it's not hard to make a mess of it. In my opinion, a sensible safeguard against "making a mess" of your life is to work at being alert to the importance of a continuous search for (more) meaning.

Unfortunately, I think many, if not most, folks unconsciously assume that M&P will come to them, without a search. Maybe they think it will be pointed out by a guru, a faith of some kind, a religious leader or, in modern times, by a celebrity, such as a seven-foot NBA, rapper-product spokesman, or "New Age" guru who sees the light of one kind or another. You, I suspect, perceive this as a pitiful situation and thank your good fortune that you know better. Unfortunately, there are a lot of folks out there not nearly so well off "cognitively speaking" as you are!

In any event, my hypothesis (the first of many to follow) is that without some kind of a conscious search process or openness to and curiosity about M&P, it is unlikely you will serendipitously come across a fulfilling sense of M&P in life, at least not to the degree that is even close to your potential in this regard. Do you tend to agree with this assertion?

M&P AND THE HEALTH CARE SYSTEM

The search for M&P in life has, of course, long attracted the attention of philosophers and theologians as well as scientists, artists, and ordinary folks. If it were to be increasingly seen as a health and wellness issue, M&P might become a national priority. I think that would be a very good thing. What do you think at this point? Should M&P be a part of the national debate on medicare and health care system reform?

Without exception, I think everybody has a well developed set of ideas about M&P for living. The problem, I suspect, is that many (if not most) are unaware of the fact that they have such ideas! It may be time to bring M&P to the forefront of conscious awareness. That is one of my purposes. Another is to encourage you to assess your current assumptions and decide if you are satisfied. In my view, ideas about M&P in life are too important to neglect. Encouraging an interest in scrutinizing specific perceptions of M&P, such as for the work you do, can lead to a lifelong interest in the subject. This quest can complement whatever interests you already have about living a healthier and happier existence. In short, the search for meaning can, in innumerable ways, make life better. That's the theory. Rather than just ask what you think in general terms, I'll give you some choices. Please check one of the following:

A. You're full of it, Don! _____
B. I couldn't agree more. _____
C. I'm not sure yet. I'll decide later. _____

One way to spark your own interest (or others') in connecting M&P and physical and psychological health is to offer a few provocative opinions. These opinions deal with the Great Questions posed moments ago, such as "What's it all about?" Here are ten such propositions that I made up, in part to get a reaction from you and a few of my friends, and in part to summarize my own thinking. The ten propositions got such a rise out of wellness leaders and practitioners that I decided to organize this book around them.

MY PROPOSITIONS—AND A FEW CAVEATS ABOUT THEM

Before I list my ten propositions, I want to repeat myself (but I'll try not to make a habit of it): I do not care in the slightest if you agree with all or any of my propositions! My intention is not to win you over to my point of view. I want you to feel excited about *your* point of view, in fact, I'd be really delighted if I stimulated you to write your own ten propositions, even if they turn out diametrically different from mine!

I made my propositions as provocative as I could, consistent with what I really believe. I did this to get your attention, make things interesting, and prod you to evaluate your own beliefs. My propositions are not important—what thoughts you generate while reflecting on them *are* important. Of course, if you agree with them (more or less), that's fine, too. All I ask is that you not use my ten propositions as the basis for a new religion!

I believe studies would show a linkage between the presence of positive, healthful lifestyle choices (i.e., a strong sense of personal responsibility, regular and vigorous exercise practices, sound nutrition, constructive attitudes for dealing with stress, and so on) and consent with all or most of my ten propositions. I believe that but, I must admit, such studies have not been done. How could they?—I just made up these propositions so the research types and foundations that fund this kind of thing have not had time to organize the requisite double-blind, cross-over trials just yet. But, I know what they will find—they'll find I'm right! One reason for my confidence is the evidence for "psychopathology" in the presence of meaninglessness as described in the psychiatric literature.[1] Belief in a grand plan in which one is assigned a role seems to be a denial of one's freedom to choose one's own way of life—and lifestyle choices. An "I'm not responsible" attitude is hardly consistent with the idea that you must invest your life with meaning (proposition one), explore possibilities (two), discover things for yourself (seven) and never stop exploring (ten).

You may want to ponder this as you go along. I feel this way because the propositions are based on my interests and pursuits as a wellness promoter and as a person trying to live an optimal wellness lifestyle. But then, many of my good friends and fellow wellness promoters and practitioners who contributed their thoughts on M&P to this effort do not agree with the propositions—and their lifestyles are just as sensible as mine. Well, almost! As suggested, consent or dissent is not my objective in listing these propositions. My objective is stimulation, to spark your interest in a few great questions. From a health perspective, my first objective is to spark your curiosity about why you're here and what you plan to do to make the most of it, including whether you will decide to adopt and maintain a positive and fulfilling lifestyle.

While consensus is not a great priority for me in fashioning ten M&P propositions, encouraging tolerance for varied positions is. I think we do best in this life when we find our own "truths." I don't think mine are particularly inspired, and I'm always suspicious when others make such claims, especially since so many "truths" of this genre are conflicting. I'm clear that mine make sense for me, but I'll cheerfully abandon any or all of them when others come along that make more sense. Nor are all propositions created equal—some seem clearly more significant than others. (My first proposition, if nothing else, is certainly more sweeping in its basic assertion than any of the others.) Once again, let me reiterate that what matters most, from your perspective, is what *you* think! The mindset you adopt on M&P will, I believe, have a significant impact on your lifestyle choices. These choices, in turn, condition the quality of your existence. In summary, I offer this list of ten propositions primarily to encourage you to think and perhaps create your own. Without further ado, here's what I think about the MOL, M&P, and a few related matters.

TEN PROPOSITIONS ABOUT M&P

1. Life is without inherent meaning; to be optimally well, you must invest life with M&P.

2. It is better to reflect on possibilities than to adhere to dogmas and creeds.

3. Most people now, as in the past, live lives that are nasty, brutal, meaningless, and short. Life need not be nasty, brutal, and meaningless. It will still be short.

4. Life's a funny proposition after all.

5. Everyone has made decisions about M&P; unfortunately, many are unaware of their choices or are uncomfortable or resistant to discussing them.

6. Everyone initially obtains his or her sense of M&P from others, usually parents. First impressions, however, get fine-tuned over time.

7. The most fulfilling insights on M&P are discovered, not revealed.

8. Although we are unique, our similarities outweigh our differences.

9. Certain expressions of M&P are quests worthy for everyone to consider.

10. The search for M&P should never end.

Each of these propositions is discussed and critiqued in the ten chapters that follow.

If you're so charged up about any of these statements that you want to get right into the heart of the matter, feel free to skip ahead to the chapter that most interests you. (You can come back to this part of the introduction anytime and not miss a thing or be confused in any way.)

If, on the other hand, you are somewhat curious as to how I came to hold some of these (supply your own adjective— "weird," "bizarre," "goofy," or "ridiculous," for example) perspectives, then stay with me for a while, right where you are.

This might be a good time to share with you how I came to adopt these propositions, to pursue M&P as part of wellness, and otherwise ended up (at least for now) with these (quite possibly peculiar) views.

MY INTEREST IN M&P

The earliest event I recall that might have been a spark lighting my interest in M&P goes back half a century, to my first encounter with death. Summers in those years were spent at the New Jersey seashore, in a cottage owned by my grandparents. We called granddad "Uncle Johnny" and, during the summer of my seventh year, Uncle Johnny was at home, dying of cancer. In order to avoid disturbing granddad, my brother and I were not allowed to play in or around the house, so I don't remember a lot about that "quiet" period. What I do remember vividly is an event which occurred after Uncle Johnny died: the funeral service. En route to the cemetery, I was allowed to ride in the front seat of the hearse, and I was able to talk with the undertaker, one of a group of people who, until that moment, were mighty mysterious to this seven-year-old.

For some reason, my parents had discouraged questions about dying, so I took advantage of the occasion to ask an "expert" some pointed questions. My recollection is that this man was kindly and talkative, but he definitely did not offer whatever answers I was looking for. Maybe he didn't want to say anything different from what I was hearing at home—I don't know. However, instead of settling matters, his evident discomfort raised my anxieties—and interests. I recall wondering what was to become of Uncle Johnny and, of course, what lay ahead for me when, albeit "a very long time from now," I ended in a similar situation.

A few other episodes that raised the standard existential puzzles can be added to the funeral of Uncle Johnny:

- religious indoctrination (particularly the news that Jesus was able to rise from the grave but I shouldn't count on it);
- the death of playmates and pets;
- encounters with a variety of astonishing fairy tales;
- radio dramas and movies; and
- family discussions, which could end abruptly if the conversation drifted into delicate areas (later, it became a game to find the borders of forbidden topical territories).

Other than my early childhood, four events or circumstances seem influential in the formation of my adult curiosities about M&P.

The first occurred just after I graduated from George Washington University (GWU). I was student body president in my senior year and had the wonderful opportunity of being in attendance in the White House Rose Garden at a reception given by President John F. Kennedy. Throughout my years at GWU, which coincided with Kennedy's presidency, I was greatly impressed by and enthusiastic about the young president. Part of this was hero worship, no doubt, since he and I were both "presidents." In any event, I thought JFK was mighty splendid and majestic, what with his beautiful wife, exciting life, sense of humor, vast power, grace, quick wit, high intelligence, and good looks. Basically, Kennedy had it all, as I saw "all," so when he was assassinated, I was not only grieved, I was reminded of life's frailty, unfairness, unpredictability, and, to a great degree, futility, even when you had "everything." A lot of my previous confidence and optimism was shaken. Feeling vulnerable and mourning, I had to deal with many moments of "what's-it-all-about" self-examination. In the course of such questioning, I started to explore meaning and purpose in a more organized manner.

Years later, three other influences reinforced these same curiosities, albeit in dramatically different ways. One was the Monty Python movie *The Meaning of Life*. Seriously. Humor is a powerful phenomenon—it's just amazing how grown men in dresses can profoundly explain things (birth, death, war, love, etc.) in such compelling ways. You just don't want to miss the scene following the organ donor sequence wherein the widow is taken on a tour of the universe—and everything is placed in true perspective. If Joe Bob (the nationally syndicated movie critic who reviews "B-grade" movies with tongue—and pen—in cheek) were writing this, he's say, "check it out." The Python movie helped me appreciate the rich dramatic and comic possibilities attendant upon the seemingly ultraserious puzzle of life's M&P. Even if I couldn't figure out the MOL, maybe there were at least some pleasantries to be experienced in tilting at this glorious windmill. Somehow, a light touch of premeditated humor in the face of the void escalated a growing fascination with the topic.

Another influence, almost as comical at times, was the constant intrigues and machinations of a range of reprehensible television preachers (and an assortment of religious leaders who didn't have the benefit of electronic ministries). Surely, you have read enough about these miscreants to appreciate how flim-flam artists prey on vulnerable people. Their victims are desperate and confused; they need neatly packaged ideas about M&P. They seem to lack the resources (education, skepticism, self-confidence, etc.) to sustain an independent quest over a lifetime. These preachers, oily and transparently bogus, led me to an early insight that still sparks my interest: an inability to find satisfying meaning in this life leads some to seek extremely simple answers, abandon reason, tolerate fools, and uncritically ingest heaps of astonishing nonsense. Of course, maybe the TV evangelists are all 100 percent correct and I'm the one without a clue. If their "truths" really are what they claim, I suppose I'll get my come-uppance soon enough. Just the same, I think I'll go with reason and take my chances.

The fourth, and most influential aspect of all, was the ever-growing interest in "spirituality" within the wellness movement. This topic deserves its own section!

SPIRITUALITY, WELLNESS, AND M&P

As the wellness movement grew in influence and sophistication, and as the scope of the concept grew well beyond the physical, the focus of attention shifted from the body (fitness, nutrition, stress management, and even mental/psychological aspects of health) to the "spiritual" dimension. At present, spirituality seems to be a notion within the wellness movement that is both highly valued and very vague. It is, of course, dominated by persons and traditions of organized religions, all of whom champion some form of higher power, usually called "God." Fortunately (from my own perspective), the varying kinds of dogma, creed, ceremony, and tradition that promote this deistic bias seem to keep each other at bay, and none predominates or at least makes dissent socially unacceptable. Yet, spirituality is a relatively new issue area within the wellness movement. Some early promoters saw spirituality as the key to wellness from the beginning, but the clear focus at the start of the movement during the late 1970s was fitness, along with nutrition, stress management, culture change, and personal responsibility. As the years passed and the movement grew exponentially, it attracted a much broader range of professionals, many outside the medical community. Today, the scope of issues encompassed seems nearly limitless. Many topics address health matters far beyond the margins of nonsickness. As mentioned, the hard-to-define area of spirituality is at the forefront of topical areas.

The rise of spirituality was probably inevitable, since health in general and wellness in particular were always described as body, mind, and spirit propositions. It just took a while to get around to the last. Nearly everyone in the health field agrees that, to be well, your lifestyle interests must go beyond a focus on being fit. Equally (or actually more) important is feeling good about your life, your work, friends, and general situation; a sound mind in a healthy body, in other words. But, there is no denying that confusion sets in when we try to get specific about the word "spirit."

In corporate and institutional wellness programs, many individuals persist in asking the spirituality questions in one form or another. Of course, it could be that this matter does not lend itself to answers. Those of us in the wellness movement given to a secular perspective favor the "no generic answers, find your own alternative" option. If we had to deal with spirituality in wellness, I personally wanted it to be as secular as possible. Then I quickly realized I had an oxymoron on my hands!

Webster's Ninth New Collegiate Dictionary offers four definitions of spirituality, all of which are religious in nature. One is "something that in ecclesiastical law belongs to the church or to a cleric as such." Two is simply "clergy," as in spirituality means "clergy." Three is "sensitivity or attachment to religious values." Four is "the quality or state of being spiritual," which of course begs the question. Thus, spirituality clearly appears to be a religious word and, unless you are doing wellness promotion in a convent or in the context of some religious purpose, it could confuse matters and maybe even divide people.

While spirituality is a fine word for people who value faith in the divine, it doesn't work quite as well for others. Yet, secularists, too, want to address matters pertaining to the inner life. I think we all care about deeper matters, from "why am I here, what's it all about," to a host of related concerns of an existential nature. These issues are equally compelling to secular and religious folks, despite their markedly different orientations. For these reasons, I settled on the oxymoronic phrase "secular spirituality." I think it's a good oxymoron. It seems to balance the conventionally "spiritual" term with a secular orientation. Addressing M&P from this outlook is, for me, a natural way to blend personal and professional interests in the health promotion movement. If someone is uncomfortable with the word "spirituality" due to its religious connotations, "secular spirituality" should make it okay. Maybe this phrase will appeal both to persons with a religious and those with a secular worldview. For those like myself, who favor an attitude of skeptical inquiry, free at least of some superstitions, creeds, and dogmas, it should be very much preferable to spirituality unadorned or unmodified.

On the other hand, for wellness educational purposes, perhaps we should pretend that the word spirit has been eliminated from the English language! (Thinking in these seemingly preposterous terms reminds me of Steve Martin's routine on how to take hostages: "Always make at least three demands, at least one of which should be totally ludicrous, as in 'I want a getaway car, a million dollars and the letter "M" eliminated from the English language!'" Then, in an audience aside, Martin would guffaw, "Hah, imagine, a getaway car!")

If we effectively excise the word "spirit" from the language (the letter "M" can stay), we might find it easier to promote discussions and explorations of M&P at the worksite and elsewhere.

In a recent edition of the *Secular Humanist Bulletin*,[2] Tom Flynn suggested that America is awash in "neospirituality," which he labeled "transcendent double-talk signifying nothing." Flynn describes how "spirit" is used by a diverse range of groups from Christian to new age "neospiritualists" in a manner synonymous with "the transcendent, which may be almost anything." He continues:

Beneath the diversity, the new creeds share a desperate conviction that there is more to life than the ordered play of matter and energy. They offer escape from what Francis Crick calls the "astonishing hypothesis": the dry view that everything we are results from chemical and electrical events inside our skulls. Neospirituality means never having to admit that a mind is one small phenomenon in a relentlessly causal universe. It means never acknowledging that in the cosmic scheme of things, we humans just don't matter all that much. Secular humanists reject the idea that the universe has an architect, much less that he, she, or it might have big plans for us. Neospiritualists seize that self-aggrandizing notion and wallow in it.... It's ... one more way Americans can turn their brains into fudge . . .[3]

Flynn concludes that spirit can carry seven mundane meanings:

It can signify life, vigor, courage, nature, intent, mood, or the sublime. Would it intolerably impoverish our language if, when we intend a mundane referent, we avoid spirit in favor of a word that says just what we mean? I think not. To prove it, I sat down with my word processor's thesaurus and in less than ten minutes compiled 95 alternatives to spirit [see box, below]. I'm sure I only scratched the surface.... Why go on using a weasel word that can only sow confusion . . . ? Let us call courage courage, call vigor vigor, and call the sublime the sublime.[4]

Here are Flynn's 95 alternatives:

95 Ways Not to Say Spirit[5]

"Spirit" in the sense of life

animation
consciousness
dash
energy
essence
feeling
spark
vitality
vivacity

"Spirit" in the sense of vigor

ardor
enthusiasm
gusto
liveliness
resolution
spunk
zeal

"Spirit" in the sense of courage

audacity
dauntlessness
determination
firmness
fortitude
grit
pluck
resolve
steadfastness
tenacity

"Spirit" in the sense of nature

character
essence
drift (as in, "You get my drift?")
gist
quintessence
substance

"Spirit" in the sense of intent

intention
meaning
purport
resolution
sense
significance

"Spirit" in the sense of mood

attitude
disposition
feeling
frame of mind
humor
temper
tenor

"Spirit" in the sense of the sublime

admirable
affecting
amazing
astonishing
attractive
charming
dazzling
elegant
elevated
enticing
excellent
exciting
exquisite
grand
harmonious
imposing
impressive
inspiring
lofty
magnificent
majestic
marvelous
matchless
moving
noble
outstanding
overwhelming
peerless
piquant
poignant
provoking
radiant
resplendent
seductive
sensual
sparkling
splendid
stately
stimulating
stirring
stupefying
superb
thrilling
touching
unsurpassed
venerable
virtuous
wonderful
wondrous

So, instead of resisting the focus on spirituality in wellness, I thought I'd join it—by terming the search for meaning and purpose secular spirituality! Of course, what resulted (as you noted from the above propositions) is not the kind of spirituality that a religious person will favor or even recognize, perhaps. But let's hope that there is room for yet another way to address the inner life. If it works for some or, better yet, stimulates nearly everybody, what's the harm?

In any event, even I would not want wellness leaders to shy away from discussions of the spiritual aspect of health. If this happened, a critical dimension of well-being would remain outside the field. In this scenario, M&P would be ignored or would remain the province of religious authorities. This would render everyone poorer "spiritually."

PROPOSITIONS AS CHOICES

The meaning of life has two quite different connotations; cosmic and terrestrial. If you are interested in the quest for a cosmic explanation of life's meaning, then you are looking for an understanding of how all human life (and yours in particular) fits into an overall coherent pattern. Lots of luck. On the other hand, you may be willing to settle for a terrestrial interpretation, a connotation of meaning wherein *you* decide on the purposes of your being. In the latter instance, meaning must be invented. This quest for transcendence can take unlimited forms (e.g., creative accomplishments, projects, concern for others) just as in cosmic systems of meaning, but it will rest on foundations that are entirely secular.

Whatever your choice, and it *is* a choice, the challenge for all of us, including cosmic seekers, seems to be, "How can I find satisfying M&P over the course of my life?"

Inasmuch as self-responsibility is the core value in the wellness concept, it should not surprise you that I favor a terrestrial approach to M&P. To be responsible in this context means you are the uncontested (in your mind) author of your destiny and ultimately accountable for your opportunities and predicaments, joys, and sufferings. A cosmic perspective, the norm for most in our culture, is based on assumptions of a grand design for the universe. Individual existence is a part of that all-encompassing purpose. Those who embrace this belief system see themselves as part of a spiritual, mythic order superior to themselves. Meaning is to be discovered via revelation.

We can and do, as adults, choose our own views of M&P. We may not call them propositions, but they are still choices about our points of existential view. In the ten chapters to follow in part two, you will be asked to evaluate the usefulness of ten propositions on M&P. Be aware that I could not have imagined any of these ideas as a young adult, or even ten years ago. First impressions are, naturally, conditioned by our parents and other formative influences. Yet, eventually the choices become our own. This is true even if we choose to adopt, word for word, the opinions and teachings of mommy, daddy, the pope, or anyone else.

As a person who believes everything is obliterated at death, and how we play, treat others, and enjoy our existence (e.g., fairly, courageously, and above all, with panache) makes all the difference, I'm delighted that these choices are mine to make. I would not want these choices made by anyone else, not even a supernatural, benevolent, and otherwise very nice being—even if I could be overwhelmed with evidence that this being were for real. As it is, all things considered, I prefer assuming responsibility for my choices, thank you very much. If you feel the same, you should enjoy the ten chapters on propositions, even if you don't agree with them!

In summary, I'll mention a curious discovery: I found biblical support for my sense that this is it, the only life we get. (However, I'd be among the first to note that such passages are easily misread, especially by me!) Still, recall Ecclesiastes on cosmic and terrestrial meaning: "All is emptiness and chasing the wind" and "For there is no doing, no learning, no wisdom in the grave where you are going." (9:7–10) Okay, neither you nor the universe will endure. In the long run, nothing is of lasting, eternal consequence, so don't let it ruin your day. Put things in perspective. I thought young Calvin of "Calvin and Hobbes" fame (Bill Watterson) captured this idea perfectly. In one of Watterson's brilliant cartoons, Calvin exclaims, "The problem with people is they don't look at the big picture," which he then proceeded to lay out for Hobbes as follows: "Eventually, we're each going to die, our species will go extinct, the sun will explode, and the universe will collapse. Existence is not only temporary, it's pointless! We're all doomed, and worse, nothing matters!" Upon hearing this, Hobbes replied, "I can see why people don't like to look at the big picture," to which Calvin responds, "Well, it puts a bad day in perspective."

Perhaps the propositions will serve the same noble purpose for you, and in the process encourage you to make the most of the time you have by choosing a lifestyle consistent with optimal enjoyment and well-being. That's what wellness is really all about.

None of this is reason for being a sourpuss. Life can be wonderful, of immense value, with great meaning and mighty purpose, if you choose to make it so, and with a little bit of luck. "Savor the moment," Rabbi Kushner (author of *When Bad Things Happen to Good People* and *When All You've Ever Wanted Isn't Enough*) urges, for "moments of our lives can be eternal without being everlasting."[6] You're here today, gone tomorrow, so *make all you can of today!* As George M. Cohan reminded us in the memorable song I adopted and worked into my fourth proposition, "Life's a very funny proposition after all!" Just don't let this fact ruin your day. Find your own M&P and you should be (reasonably) happy.

ASSUMPTIONS ABOUT THE TEN PROPOSITIONS

Not all my assumptions were conscious, I suppose, but of those that were, some comments seem appropriate before launching into these chapters.

One prime assumption is that the process of pondering M&P is likely to excite insights on a variety of important "quality of life" issues. Another is that a position of deliberate openness to a range of possibilities adds to the chances for optimal health and the maximum enjoyment of life. I still believe these two, and will develop these ideas in the chapters to come. You can decide for yourself if each is a sensible assumption as you work your way through.

Here are a few other assumptions I found helpful in shaping the ten propositions:

- The search for M&P belongs at the top of the agenda in institutional health promotion programs. Approached with diplomacy and sensitivity, in a way that makes a fascinating topic accessible to all, it seems a likely candidate for wellness issue number one. What else can compare? Cholesterol levels? Body fat? Exercise?

- The promotion of a search for M&P in life in a wellness context is best conducted as a secular pursuit, even by those who are religious. This is an era of diversity, not just in racial and ethnic terms but ideological diversity, as well. Appeal to the widest possible audience—those with religious orientations can pursue these interests in like-minded associations beyond the workplace.

- The dialogue on M&P is best conducted in a manner characterized by respect for scientific evidence grounded in human understanding and reason. However, the focus should never be on answers. Questions and curiosities are much more attractive—and agreeable.

- M&P, much like happiness, is probably not an objective to be reached as much as a process to value. Viktor Frankl (author of *Man's Search for Meaning*) often noted that happiness ensued from good work; it rarely resulted from a direct quest for happiness itself.

- A healthy lifestyle, a commitment to wellness values and other inclinations toward optimal functioning complement a search for added M&P. The best sense of M&P in life is not likely to entail "being healthy" for most thoughtful people, although optimal health is a fine state for as long as it can be maintained. Rather, a continual openness to and interest in M&P will prove to be its own reward, and that goes deeper than health, which is a fleeting state under the best of circumstances, and requires much good fortune.

- As noted in the final proposition, the quest for M&P in life never ends; similarly, don't expect "Eureka-type" discoveries. These ideas take time to settle in, to percolate, and lead to something else. Try to resist the urge to decide where you stand until you have had plenty of time to look around, get your bearings, and develop confidence in the lay of the land.

- Contrary to the popular aphorism, when all is said and done, it is likely that more, much more, will be *done* than *said*. By this, I mean that life does and will go on whether we are satisfied with our theories on M&P or not.

We must do what needs to be done before we have all the information we'd like to have. Life sometimes forces us into a

"Ready, Fire, Aim" mentality. Even with a predisposition to think and discuss M&P, there are too few opportunities for *saying* what we think to ourselves (self-talk) or others and too many demands for *doing* whatever is or seems to be required to get on with life.

Finally, I assumed that, if I were going to commit myself to a lengthy process of research and writing a book on M&P, I should improve my organizational abilities! The reason I came to this assumption is that I misplaced the name of the sender of the very first letter I received from a wellness promoter who knew of my interest in this topic. On the day it arrived, I typed these words on my computer from the letter:

Dear Don:

Your upcoming book sounds very intriguing. I think we all ponder "the meaning of life," some of us more than others. We should not be concerned with finding *the* meaning of life for it is a mystery and meant to stay that way. Rather, we should concern ourselves with meaningful pursuits. Then, at the end of our life, when we look back on our accomplishments, our life will have meaning.

It is a wise statement and a great sendoff into the ten chapters in Part Two that follow. And, as you can tell from what I wrote so far, one that influenced me. Unfortunately, I misplaced the letter and consequently have no way of knowing the identity of the author! I have to credit "anonymous" with this insight. But, now I'm better organized! If the writer of these words reads this, I hope she or he will accept my humble apologies—and thanks. To enjoy the ten propositions—and the letters I did not lose, please continue to Part Two straight ahead.

Enjoy.

NOTES

1. See, for example, the discussion of meaninglessness and physical disease in chapter 6 (pp. 273–76) and psychotherapy in chapter 11 (pp. 461–83) of *Existential Psychotherapy* by Irvin D. Yalom (New York: Basic Books, 1980).

2. Tom Flynn, "We Need Some Exorcise!" Reprinted by permission from *Secular Humanist Bulletin*, 10, no. 3 (Fall 1994): 6.

3. Ibid.

4. Ibid., p. 7.

5. Tom Flynn, "95 Ways Not to Say Spirit," *Secular Humanist Bulletin*, 10, no. 3 (Fall 1994): 6.

6. Harold Kushner, *When All You've Ever Wanted Isn't Enough: The Search for a Life That Matters* (New York: Pocket Books, 1986), p. 141.

Part Two

Ten Propositions about Meaning and Purpose

1

Proposition One

Life Is without Inherent Meaning; To Be Optimally Well You Must Invest Life with Meaning and Purpose.

"Smile! Be happy! Enjoy life! Be creative! Cry! Laugh! Hug somebody! Dream! Explore new ideas! Be yourself! Eat well!" (Message at the bottom of the breakfast and lunch menu at The Wooden Chair, a restaurant in Stevens Point, Wisconsin, a town known as the "Mecca" of the wellness movement.)

INTRODUCTION

This initial proposition, "Life is without inherent meaning; to be optimally well you must invest life with M&P," may seem an odd paradox to you at first. It makes perfect sense to me, but then, it should—I wrote it! It is precisely because I do not believe in a cosmic, all-encompassing meaning of life that I feel so strongly that we must invest our time on Earth exploring our own meanings and purposes. From my standpoint as both a wellness seeker and a professional promoter of this artful and healthy lifestyle, I think it's imperative. I am convinced doing so can be enjoyable, exciting, and endlessly rewarding. On the other hand, I realize that it may not work for you—and you are the best judge of any M&P proposition. Thus, my goal in this chapter and those to follow is to make the process, the idea of examining M&P options, as interesting and desirable as possible. That's one reason I have so many opinions to share with you courtesy of the wellness leaders—if my propositions don't help or agree with you, maybe somebody else's will!

In this chapter, I'll do my best to get you to agree only with the idea that seeking M&P is worth your efforts; I will not make any effort to tell you what your M&P should look like. One reason for this strategy is that I haven't a clue how to do this; another is that it's none of my business. And now, let me go on a bit about this meaningless existence I'm stuck with—and how I am (and a few of my wellness-oriented colleagues are) trying to give life some meaning and a bit of purpose.

A FEW WORDS ABOUT INHERENT OR "COSMIC" MEANING

A search for inherent meaning, for the meaning of life, is a cosmic perspective. In my view, as you surely know by now, this is futile, possibly frustrating, and potentially dangerous. Among other perils, you could end up in a cult or a loony bin! There are a lot of zealots of all kinds who would love to give you the answer to the MOL and take your money and your brain at the same time! Many cults in America have been accused of this, and in the Middle East, for example, there are mullahs (quasi-clerical Muslims trained in the law and doctrine of that faith) who distort the Islamic religion by convincing desperate, ill-informed, and abused youngsters that they can line up next to Allah in the next life (with seventy virgins to boot) by driving a car bomb into Israelis, thereby becoming a martyr.[1]

This first proposition, that there is no universal meaning of life, that we are insignificant cosmic accidents, except to ourselves, is widely shared by others with a secular orientation like my own. Carl Sagan put it this way: "We are the custodians of life's meaning. We would prefer it to be otherwise, of course, but there is no compelling evidence for a cosmic parent who will care for us and save us from ourselves. It is up to us."[2] Sagan's view was the predominant reaction I obtained from wellness promoters and practitioners, but that may be just because I heard from those who tended to agree with me. Well, who knows? What matters is what you think about this idea and how you might develop some ideas for your own use, and maybe to use with others, while exploring M&P.

Part of the quest for meaning, I think, is trying to find and then developing your passions. What is it you really care to do? What kind of work would provide a showcase for your talents? Answer these and similar questions and you'll be close to an understanding of your ways of finding meaning. Finding and cultivating one or more passions seems to me a reliable way to make life meaningful.

COMMENTS BY WELLNESS PROMOTERS

The reactions from wellness leaders to this and the other propositions were not as varied as I would have expected, although, as I've noted, it could be that those who shared my predispositions tended to be the ones who contacted me. In the following pages, I want to give you a broad picture of the scope of the responses to this proposition. The first set of comments are basically extensions of the proposition; the next set are dissents from it. Try to hold off the tendency to adopt or settle on one or more of the comments until you've had a chance to review the entire package of reactions. Then I'll ask you some questions and give you a few tips for working with this kind of material, if you find it useful or enjoyable to do so in some special context. You may find that facilitating explorations of M&P for coworkers, students, and others to be a fascinating and worthwhile experience.

Generally Supportive Observations

Wendy Shore of Leesburg, for one, seemed to concur with the first proposition about M&P. Here's what Wendy had to say:

> I don't think there is a meaning of life, either. There are many things that can give meaning to life, and the wonderful part is we get to choose. We can choose whether to see ourselves as meaningful and what to do to make our lives meaningful. We can choose to judge other's choices and we can have lots of fun being critical or admiring those choices. We can choose whether to spend our lives exercising, laughing, and breathing fresh air, or being bitter, blaming, and doing everything possible to make our bodies uncomfortable. We can choose to have a family and love them a lot, or have a family and be irritated by them a lot. We can choose not to have a family at all. We can choose to spend our working hours at a job that challenges us or at one that makes us feel very comfortable by being the same every day. We can choose whether to seek, give, avoid, or ignore love. We can choose

never to leave home, or to travel so much we barely remember where home is. As in the nursery rhyme, "The world is so full of a number of things, I am sure we should all be as happy as kings." What life is most full of is choices—and choices can give meaning to life.

Do you feel free to choose? If so, do you exercise these choices and opportunities daily? Sometimes, people get stuck in a rut of their own making, and lose the capacity for choice. How are you doing in this regard? What's your reaction to Wendy's comments?

One of my dear friends, Alan Tranter of Perth, Western Australia, a top administrator of a sports and recreation agency, thinks we should spend little or no time seeking a cosmic idea of the MOL and more time simply doing what we do well, which seems pretty consistent with what has been discussed so far. Here are Alan's words (without the funny accent):

> There is no such thing as "the" meaning of life but there are many ways of managing every situation. Try to be a hero and you will end up looking like a [fool]; do all the little things well and you could be a hero. Oh, how we try to be the center of attention. Most times it fails! Concentrate on being very good at what you do and it is just possible that the stage could be yours.

I've managed to look foolish many times when being a hero was the last thing on my mind, but I think Alan has a point. We don't have to do everything well, or heroically. Isn't it a relief to know that?

Don Kemper of Boise, Idaho hints that taking ourselves too seriously may be an easily eliminated source of stress. Don writes that meaning may lurk in the little pleasures missed by adults but self-evident to a child. In response to my question "What's it all about?" Don offered this:

> To get up each morning with hope. To live each day with direction. To go to bed each night with satisfaction. Or, as my daughter said at age five, when asked, "What is the most important thing in the world?" "Breakfast!"

I guess I'm not the first to notice that we can learn from our children, if we're paying attention at the right times.

Of course, some adults are pretty bright about these sorts of things, too. Susan B. Frampton of Manchester, Connecticut explained why she finds life lacking inherent meaning—and why we must create it:

> How can we address the question of the meaning and purpose of our lives? How do we discover the meaning of anything, for that matter? Imagine we are archaeologists in an unknown land, and in our travels we stumble upon something we have never encountered before. This "something" is incredibly complex, at the same time wonderful and terrible in its magnificent complexity. We want desperately to discover its M&P. We ask ourselves, "What is the meaning of this grand and frightening thing?" We look around the area in which it is situated and ask "What relationships does it have to other elements in its environment? Is it a part of something else?" We pick it up and turn it over and wonder "What does it do? How does it function? Is there some unique contribution made by its existence?" These same questions can help us to discover the M&P of our own complex, wonderful, and sometimes terrible lives. There is no universal and inherent life purpose shared by all human beings. The M&P of our lives evolves over our lifespan. It is the measure of our re-

lationships with our families, our friends, our communities, our society, and our planet. It is the sum of all that we do and the contributions we make during our time here. We are not born into a life of M&P, we are instead born with the capacity and potential to achieve such a life. The ultimate challenge for each person is the creation, day by day, of a life that holds M&P within it; M&P that breathes life into our existence and the existence of our companions, fire into our hearts and the hearts of those we love, music and laughter in our souls and the souls of those we touch. What is the M&P of our lives? Why, to create meaningful and purposeful existences, of course!

John Bailiff of Stevens Point, Wisconsin also believes that meaning is invented by the way we live our lives:

Last year, a woman asked me what meaning I thought life had. I replied that life doesn't have meaning, it gets meaning. What I meant was that my life acquires its meaning in the course of my living it, in the course of the choices, decisions, discoveries I make. Of course, this implies that my life's meaning is retrospective. I learn its meaning only by looking back. "Life can only be understood backwards," as Kierkegaard remarked. "Unfortunately," he added, "it must be lived forwards."

Charles Cochrane of Subiaco, Western Australia, who billed himself as a "silent Australian philosopher," sent blank pages—and insisted that I print his unexpurgated version of the MOL. I didn't, of course, assuming the publisher would not have gone for the idea of printing blank pages as an entry. This, of course, was Australian humor, Charles's way of saying "A meaning? Get real!" a variant, I suppose, of the remark attributed to

Gertrude Stein, to wit: "There ain't no answer, there never has been an answer, and there never will be an answer and *that's* the answer!'

Charles and I discussed this proposition and its implications many times since the day we met at a National Wellness Conference in 1985, during many tours of Australia conducting wellness programs, last year at a Dallas Cowboys football game, and most recently in a coffee shop in Perth five months before he passed away in May 1995. He was an iconoclastic and witty free-thinker, a warm-spirited guy, and a very supportive friend.

Peter Gianoli, also of Western Australia (Perth), expressed a view much like Charles's. Peter responded to my MOL question with two questions of his own: "When my time is up in this life I want to answer 'Yes' to the following questions: 'Did you bring happiness into the world?' and 'Did you find happiness in the world?' This is what gives me meaning and purpose."

For Tom Ferguson of Austin, Texas, the meaning of life is to find your mission and then make it happen. Gloria Kotecki of South Milwaukee invents meaning in a way that Viktor Frankl would endorse, namely, through service to others. Here's how Gloria put it: "For me, the MOL is to help others in any way I can. This leads to peace of mind and heart even when the world is falling apart around me."

Kathy Miculka of Dallas had the same theme when she wrote that everyone must make it up—and be quick about it: "Life's purpose? If you don't have one, make one up! Get started, now. You are guaranteed to get immediate feedback. Pay attention and use the information to refine your ideas."

Even those who agreed had a wide range of ways to go about it, as witnessed by the somewhat aggressive or perhaps mystical interpretation by Rod Raymond of Duluth, Minnesota: "The purpose of life can have several meanings, but to me it is actively and passionately listening to the warrior that exists within while fulfilling the dynamic needs of the body, mind, and spirit."

Denise P. Padilla of Fort Collins, Colorado went on a round-about explanation and came back to the notion of passion:

What is the MOL? Actually, the question is or should be "What meaning do and can I give to life?" Living life is a process, the reason why we are here. This process is one of discovery, expression, and responsibility. It involves the discovery of who you are, what you are, what motivates you, and how you express it all in what you think, say, and do. It is learning and teaching, smelling a flower, riding a bike, climbing a mountain, listening to music, dancing, laughing, crying, creating, daydreaming, sharing, connecting with others, holding hands, wishing on a star, and so on. It is finding your passion in life. These things honor and develop who you are mentally, physically, emotionally, and spiritually—the whole person. The meaning of life is how you choose to express it. It's up to you. Here it is, what are you doing with it? As you have this human experience, keep it light. Remember that to laugh is just as important as finishing the report on time, keeping your body healthy, and honoring your spiritual connection.

Occasionally ask yourself, "What are my priorities? If I had six months to live, would my priorities change or would I continue doing what I'm doing?" Your response tells you what you need to know to focus on genuine living. Remember, the best question is not "Why am I here?" That's a done deal. Rather, decide what you are going to do while you are here and make a commitment, to yourself, to do it. Wellness is not about disease, it is about living and *you* decide how you are going to live.

Carol R. Filkins of Indianapolis finds M&P in giving and receiving as much love and joy as possible:

> When I view my purpose in life as to give and receive love then everything else gets put into proper perspective in my work and personal life. When I don't do this I end up focusing on that which is immediate rather than important. The way I see it, the problems around us aren't the result of too much bad in the world but of not enough good, not enough love. I can make a difference by providing love and joy where I can. When I'm living this philosophy I feel my life has meaning and purpose.

By now, I'm sure you can sense that even when someone concurs with a proposition, the nature of that consensus can go all over the track.

Roger Plant of Mount Pleasant, Western Australia, expressed a view that seemed typical of Australian wellness promoters, much more so than is true of their American counterparts, in readily consenting to the absence of cosmic purpose:

> There are two quotes which I find comforting from time to time. One is by Shakespeare: "Life's but . . . a tale told by an idiot, full of sound and fury signifying nothing" (*Macbeth,* Act 5, Scene 5); the other is unattributed (I heard it watching a documentary on the life of [Friedrich] Engels), namely, "The meaning of life lies solely in life itself."

Edwin Lee Morris of Franklin, North Carolina sees the fact of our existence as reason enough to make the most of it:

> I once asked a wise philosopher, "Why are we here?" The answer contained more insight than I understood at the time.

His answer was "Why Not?" What he was saying was that although we can think, reason, and search as wise men have done for centuries, we will never know for certain why we are here. We cannot know the absolute meaning of life or even if there is meaning to life. The search, however, is extremely important because the search itself has value. The search helps us come closer to finding meaning in life. Also, by experiencing the power of nature, beauty in the world, or otherwise sensing the creative energy of someone or something else, we find value and meaning. Perhaps the best way to find our special M&P in life is to become part of the creative process. Thus, we often find life-long meaning by finding our mission or purpose in life. We can find this not by some mystical vision but by understanding our own talents and skills. In these expressions we find joy. We use our talents and skills in ways that are fulfilling and useful in the world.

The secret is that it is totally up to us to find that which gives us this joy. One person may find this meaning by using his/her skill and talents as a physician, another as a teacher, and so on. Others would find the same roles boring and devoid of meaning and would thus feel trapped doing such things. Someone once asked a world-class chess champion what was the best move in chess. Of course, there is no best move in chess because everything depends on where the other player is. Likewise, there is no single meaning in life for everyone because we are all situated differently. But, we can all find meaning by using our situation and unique skills and interests. In this way, we flow in a great river of universal creation. When we are immersed in this stream of creative life energy, we are able to experience the meaning of our own lives. If we really get stuck on finding the answer to "Why are we here?" we can always take a cold shower and respond, "Why not?"

Jay N. Eacker of Walla Walla, Washington noted that not only is life without meaning but we could not know what the meaning is even if there were inherent meaning:

> [L]ife may very well have no meaning except for . . . that [which] we humans give to it. . . . [L]ife is what we make of it, and one of the things that we can make of it is to test the limits of our physical and intellectual capabilities. In the words of Henry David Thoreau on Walden Pond, "Who knows the limits of human capabilities, so little has been tried?"
>
> One link between the wellness idea and M&P might tie into this notion of "limit testing." Wouldn't you agree that in order to test your limits, you must be physically fit? After all, an unfit body places limits on what we can do. In other words, the limits of our physical and intellectual capabilities cannot be tested unless or until we are physically fit. . . . I do not know that I have tested the full limits of my physical and intellectual capabilities but, apparently, that it is the meaning that life has for me; it is one meaning of life.

Jill Shanks of Saskatoon, Saskatchewan, suggests we can find, invent, and otherwise create M&P by writing our own stories, a commitment that requires an alignment of passions, energies, and actions with chosen meanings:

> When you take time to think about things like the meaning of life, you begin to ask yourself questions. "Am I happy with my life? Has my life M&P? Am I doing what fulfills me? Why do I have a deep aching of something missing?" If you don't come back with strong, concrete answers, you know you have to do some serious thinking, come up with answers and take some action. I believe that life is without inherent meaning, that it's for you to define.
>
> How to go about it? For some, M&P is defined from child-

hood, so no need to bother! It just is. For these people, all life experiences seem geared for assigned purposes. They know what they are meant to do. For the rest of us, we must work harder to find and fulfill our purpose(s). For me, it's been a long search. I have finally come to the realization that I must go back, find the lost inner child and then my life purpose will be revealed. Finding your inner child brings you back in touch with your real self. This journey takes you past the self you portray in everyday life, beyond the defense mechanisms you have set up to the little child seeing and experiencing the world for the first time. Find that feeling of laughter, freedom, and joy in everything and your passions will be revealed.

A tool to help you find that inner child is a journal. Write out your thoughts and feelings. Go back to your child time, and journey through your life. Celebrate your history, and celebrate your life! All this means you must take a mythic journey, via writing your story! This mythic journey leads to your M&P in life. When your passions, energies, and actions are all directed toward your M&P, your body/mind and spirit will be congruent and your life will be fulfilled.

Frank A. Roberts of Fairfax, Virginia, comments in another way:

As an existentialist, I'm in total agreement with you that life is without inherent meaning and that rigid dogmas serve only to reinforce that scared, childlike and dependent part of us that magically believes that mindless obedience will protect us from all sorts of painful consequences, including that of the "angst" of free and independent thought and decision.

One of the original leaders of the wellness movement, physician John Travis, reacted to this initial proposition in a memorable fashion with these words:

I concur heartily with all ten propositions. Your premises support my own findings. Of the eleven questionnaires we used for wellness evaluations in the late 1970s, the "Purpose in Life Test" was the most powerful. It opened up more discussion than all the others put together. That finding led to my later concluding the *Wellness Workbook* with chapters on finding meaning and "transcending"—a safe way to avoid the then taboo "S" word—spirituality.

Don Kemper of Boise used his wit to put his reactions to the propositions (in addition to sharing his five-year-old daughter's conclusion noted a moment ago) into a poem:

> I read the propositions with the hope of being whole
> I searched my head for meaning,
> But I wasn't on a roll.
> I tried each one for wisdom,
> I tried each one for grace,
> I tried each one while jogging,
> At a very stately pace.
> Yet all that I could answer,
> When I asked which one for me,
> Was it's often harder thinking,
> When you really have to pee.

I want to conclude this summary of supportive comments about the first proposition with the commentary provided by my partner and best mate from Down Under, Grant Donovan. It took a long time to get a response from Grant, but when he finally took a stand, it was worth the wait: "Putting all that time into improving oneself, being the best you can be—then dying. It doesn't seem right. If there is a God, which I seriously doubt, then he certainly has wasted youth on the young." As to the first proposition, Grant quoted Samuel Butler: "the hen is only the egg's way of making another egg." But, he elaborated:

> I believe that the gene is the MOL and is there for no other reason than it is there. Larger life forms exist only as gene carriers. This is our true purpose in life. Nothing more, nothing less. I believe Phillip Adams [former columnist for *The Australian* newspaper and *The Bulletin* magazine] when he advises "the cosmos comes and goes in a vast, endless oscillation in which the birth and death of galaxies are of no more consequence than the failure of a few 40-watt light globes." All life is totally meaningless. There is no MOL, no destiny, no author.

Grant holds the MOL, as I do, to be purely subjective:

> [MOL] is one big Rorschach blot with every person seeing something different. We assign meaning and reasons to everything that happens and are always on the lookout for moral messages. But, as Steven Jay Gould says, "there are no moral messages in nature . . . it is as we find it, as fascinating as can be."
>
> So, I am not depressed that there is no MOL. Our temporal self-importance makes certain that life is challenging and interesting at times . . . [and] full of wonderful contradictions, delusions and paradoxes. It's a fun place to carry a few genes. I believe that people should be able to do what they like, no matter how silly. That chaotic logic is best, life self-assembles, and wellness comes from emergent states. I believe the nuclear bomb will go off, again and again. That humans will pollute the environment and become extinct but the DNA will survive.*

---

*One alert reviewer of this commentary wrote in the margin of the manuscript: "If human DNA survives, then humans wouldn't truly be extinct, would they?" I asked Donovan about this, to which he replied, "Hey, the DNA can survive without ever manifesting a human life form again. She's technically right, but I've got the moral high ground."

That progress is an aberration of science and business. I like randomness, and the idea that I am happy and healthy because I accept the chance nature of being. I think Elizabeth Kübler-Ross is right about acceptance. It leaves the mind free to enjoy and learn.

I like thinking and reviewing ideas. I enjoy tentative conclusions and find it interesting and exciting to speculate. I think unresolved cognitive dissonance is healthy, provided you enjoy thought talk. I believe people in power are very ordinary and unnecessary. That war is a waste of time, money, and people. That greed is a product of imprisoned beliefs. And, that people believe too much in believing. I like the thought of death because, as Phillip Adams writes, "How can we fear something that we know so well? We know what death looks, feels, and smells like because we have all been dead for billions of years. If you want to know what death is like, just think back to a few years before you were born. Death's exactly the same thing."

So, coming to terms with one's own mortality is not really that hard. Life comes and goes. You are born one day, die the next, and in between you can either enjoy yourself or develop your neurosis. It is up to you! I like the wellness idea because it encourages self-responsibility. It gets me thinking positive thoughts, whatever they are! And, it provides a forum in which randomness and mechanistic reductionism can coexist.

Wellness is a fun philosophy. It embraces divergent thought processes on the pathway to health. It helps set rules, like wearing seatbelts. It promotes personal excellence and heroic deeds. The wellness movement even possesses a series of models and charts which we can all happily live by. I think these models and philosophies are interesting but I do not think they are the answer. I enjoy the thought that there is no answer. No meaning. That we are here for The Game. We give life our own meaning and that every person's meaning is different and valid. No right or wrong, true or false, but just different.

DNA rules. OK?

Well, it's certainly okay with me. You, dear reader, can decide if it's okay with you and, if it's not, choose something else.

It's amazing how different we are, isn't it? Here are comments from those in the wellness field who did not feel very supportive of the first proposition.

Dissents from the First Proposition

If you are familiar with or oriented toward a Zenlike outlook, you might enjoy the remarks contributed by Carol Garzona, who suggested that the answers to the three great questions, "Why am I here?" "Where am I going?" and "How do I get there?" lie dormant within us. Once these questions are asked, they cannot be unasked. But the timing of the revelation is not in our hands. It is a "cosmic timing" which we don't know anything about and over which we have zero control:

> There's a story about a guy who goes to a sadhu [a Hindu mendicant ascetic] down by the river and asks him, "How do I find M&P?" The sadhu takes him by the hair and pushes him under the water and holds him there for two minutes. Finally, the sadhu lets him up for air. Then he says, "When you want to find M&P as much as you wanted to find oxygen, then *it* will find you!"

Sandra Martin of St. Louis was not quite so subtle in suggesting that this proposition did not resonate at all with her:

I strongly disagree. I have a strong sense of faith that there is
a higher power or creator of what seems at times a morass.
That higher power created a rhythm and reason for all creation. Only S/He has the capacity to fully understand the
whole picture, but each of us plays a part.

In a similar vein, Andrea Frank of Wauwatosa, Wisconsin,
who calls herself a "weaver" of a spiritual wellness network
within the wellness movement, took exception to my early use
of the term "wellness spirituality" (since abandoned for good
cause, as noted): "Try as I might, I just couldn't find the 'spirit'
in your propositions for wellness spirituality. (Perhaps that is
how you intended it?) [It is, of course, but Andrea had no way
of knowing this at the time.] Near as I can tell, the propositions
might better fit the categories of wellness existentialism or wellness nihilism."

Andrea then pointed out that some of the tenets of nihilism
and existentialism seemed, in her opinion, to mimic various of
the ten propositions. Her conclusions seemed a bit of a semantic difference to me but not everybody feels this way. Many
of the wellness promoters (those with e-mail) had a chance to
see what others had written, which sometimes led to comments
on the commentaries. John Bailiff, a professor emeritus of philosophy quoted earlier in this chapter, took exception to Andrea's use of the term nihilism:

She's wrong! Nihilism is actually the obverse of absolutism: if
there's no absolute meaning, then everything is meaningless. In other words, nihilism is the response of disillusioned
absolutists. (Nietzsche pointed this out in his *Genealogy of
Morals* [1885] and noted it would be the scourge of the twentieth century. He was right.) Your position . . . is the contrary

of nihilism: since there is no *necessary* meaning, life is infi-
nitely open to the *generation* of meaning.

One philosophical suggestion: you might achieve more
resonance by acknowledging that human effort regularly
fails; a good many things can't be given a positive or affirmative meaning. Life can and will go on, but much can be lost
unavoidably and irretrievably. This is the secret point of com-
edy, of course.

Andrea went on to comment on additional propositions
covered in the coming chapters. Her theme is lack of belief in
inherent meaning, so I'll insert Andrea's comments at this
point since we're on the subject:

When I read your propositions on M&P, I interpreted your
worldview as purely secular (pertaining to the world or to
things not spiritual or sacred). I assume that is as you intended it, since you recently commented to me that you are
interested in eliminating the word spirituality from all associations with wellness. You said, "It is a religious word with
connotations and definitions associated with religion; there
are better terms for health promotion purposes." OK, that's
your worldview. And who's to say that your worldview is wrong
and mine is right (or vice versa)? . . .

That said, I just can't understand your decision to pair the
word wellness with the word spirituality. Since your secular
propositions exclude the spiritual, wellness spirituality (at
least the way you use the term) becomes an oxymoron.

As noted previously, I agree with Andrea on most of this:

I'm sure it's no surprise to you that I have a very different view
of spiritual wellness and MOL. There are those of us in the

wellness movement who believe it is time to spiritualize wellness. This doesn't mean cramming religion or religious beliefs down other people's throats. I want to reiterate that spiritual is not necessarily a religious word, nor does it inherently carry religious overtones. Believing in God or experiencing a sense of the Holy does not require going to church. In my Webster's, spiritual refers to the existence of an incorporeal soul as bestowed by a deity. Spirituality makes a distinction between the mortal body and the immortal part of a person which has no physical or material reality. So what does this all have to do with M&P? It seems to me that the search for the MOL as you describe it is a secular pursuit. Those seeking the MOL ask, "How can I give my life meaning? What should I be doing to find the MOL?" Finding the meaning of life is a quest—an end to be pursued—an achievement—the triumph of finding the Holy Grail! (A secular holy grail, at least.) Yet, when we ask, what is the MOL—my life—any life—are we chasing the wind? What if there is no answer to the MOL? Perhaps by the very act of seeking meaning and purpose in life, life's meaning and purpose eludes us.

Andrea then concludes with a biblical passage, the sentiments of which I heartily agree:

I denied myself nothing my eyes desired, I refused my heart no pleasure. My heart took delight in all my work, and this was the reward for all my labor. Yet, when I surveyed all that my hands had done and what I had toiled to achieve, everything was meaningless, a chasing after the wind; nothing was gained under the sun. "Meaningless! Meaningless!" says the Teacher. "Utterly meaningless! Everything is meaningless."

Ecclesiastes (10:3)

I shared a draft version of this chapter with a physician friend, Mort Orman of Baltimore. Mort's comment to the above contribution was one I thought should be included:

While reading Andrea Frank's comments, and particularly her biblical passage that you quoted, I was reminded of a powerful personal experience I had with M&P about fifteen years ago. I had just discovered the joy of long-distance running after years and years of absolutely hating running. I was especially proud of my new-found ability to give my word to myself every day about running and then keep my word no matter what sorts of unforseen things (emergencies, rain, snow, colds, etc.) tried to defeat me. I was having a blast! I had just run my first marathon and had been training for months to run my second one in Boston. About three weeks before the race, I went to dinner with a bunch of friends and was quietly bragging about my self-satisfaction at keeping my word, day-in, day-out for more than a year! One of the people at the table, who was somewhat philosophically inclined, said, "You know, Mort, it really doesn't mean anything whether you keep your word or not." Well, you know what? I had to agree with him. I was so happy about my recent accomplishments that I had forgotten the truth that it really is all meaningless. Boy, was I emotionally devastated . . . I couldn't even run the next day! All the air was gone from my balloon. It was all meaningless! So why was I going out there every day like it meant something? It was all a big illusion, and I had fallen for it hook, line, and sinker. I want you to know that I almost canceled out on the race. It took me almost a week before I finally emerged from my emotional funk. How did I do it? I finally realized, "Hey, so what if it doesn't really mean anything? *It means something to me,* so I'm going to keep on doing it, and I'm going to keep on *creating positive meaning* for myself."

Fifteen years later, I'm still having a ball keeping my word to myself. I've now run five marathons and over 20,000 miles. I've taught hundreds of people how to transform their relationship to running and other forms of exercise. I'll probably write a book on the subject some day. And you know what— I'm very clear that none of it means anything—really. It's no more meaningful than getting fat and sipping mint juleps at the beach. To each his/her own passions!

Before leaving this theme, I want to offer one more word from Andrea (well, quite a few words, actually), because her views are provocative, interesting, persuasive, and otherwise worthy of pondering, despite the fact that her opinions are (a little bit) different from mine!

What if our task is not to seek meaning, but being called just to *be*—to bask in the *revelation* of the mystery inherent within life itself . . . to live in the wonder and awe of created being . . . to acknowledge the miracle of "I am" as a created being along with the miracle of other created beings? Life, then, has no meaning, because life *is* its own meaning.

And so, the question is not, "What is the MOL?" but "How should life be lived knowing that the MOL is found purely within the living of it?" So what then? Are we called to be inert blobs . . . recluses endlessly chanting "Om" in front of some religious icon? No! Instead, this revelation calls us to be our best selves . . . to be fully alive . . . to celebrate life in all its dimensions—work, play, and being. Spiritual wellness occurs when we live in the revelation that everything we do in life is an offering to the miracle of all created being. . . . Finding M&P is an individual quest, but it is a quest which we all share, and one whose answers, for some of us, lie more in the realm of the transcendent than in the imminent.

The point I'm trying to make here is that the only MOL is that all life is a spiritual gift which emanates from a transcendent source and that living life well—with respect, gratitude, joy, and awe of the Great Mystery—provides it's own meaning.

Andrea added a comment upon learning of the death of Charles Cochrane; this too may be of interest:

> I was sorry to read about your friend in Australia who died recently. I think discovering the meaning of life is an easier thing to do than discovering the meaning of death and the loss of people and other living things we love. Good friends are hard to come by. I'm sure he will be sorely missed.

Jay Eacker (mentioned earlier) said something else of interest here:

> We cannot know that life is without inherent meaning; to be optimally well, you must invent meaning and purpose. To know that life is without inherent meaning poses the same kind of problem as knowing that life has meaning and, since it is we humans who claim to know, we cannot know the thing in itself or what Immanuel Kant referred to as the *"ding an sich"**; we cannot know something apart from our own understanding.

Deb Jones of Vancouver added yet another gentle dissent:

---

*This is a German phrase that means simply "the thing in itself." We cannot know the thing in itself or as it is apart from us. We can only know things in relation to ourselves.

I do not believe that life is without meaning, but sometimes that meaning is difficult to find and, of course, is different for each of us. My mom always said "things happen for a reason." I think many things do, yet it's difficult to figure out what the reason is at the time. For example, why is it that after something really awful happens to us (that we can't understand at the time) things often turn out better because of a change we made due to the tragedy?

I give the last word on this proposition to Jane Myers, who tactfully suggested that if this and the other propositions seem sensible, then they are just fine, for me (or anyone else who chooses to agree with them!): "Your propositions reflect a secular view of what I call spirituality. While I may not agree with all of them for myself, from an existential perspective I fully agree with all of them for you!" That's pretty much what I hope these comments will spark for you—a set of working or "draft edition" ideas that you write that you will fully agree with— and be guided by as you look for new insights all the time.

Let's take a moment to look a bit closer at this wellness concept I've been going on about for quite a while now.

WHAT TO MAKE OF IT ALL

Much has been written about the wellness concept in the past decade, but the public still has little awareness of the term. This might be a good time, in the face of my assertion that life is meaningless, to ask what, exactly, is wellness—and does it really matter? I'll start by offering a commentary on what wellness is *not* about, then I'll summarize what I think it is or should be about. This may be of interest as you ponder the next nine propositions and particularly when you think about about practical ways to utilize the ideas for your benefit and for others, as well.

It may be helpful to start with a few words about *what wellness is not*. For starters, it is not a panacea or any kind of a quick fix. What's more, it is not easy. Of course, it is not sacred either and, thank goodness, it is not a religion. For this, we should be grateful. Since it's not a religion, there is no heaven to be lost or hell to pay. There is no sin, no miracles, and no guilt—in place of the latter you'll find a strong case for an ethic of personal responsibility. As a nonreligion, the concept has no sacraments, procedures for nominating or electing lifestyle, or other forms of saints. Wellness lacks rituals, it is not dogmatic and there is nothing sanctimonious about it. As you have guessed, it is not a cult, has no creed, and its most skilled promoters do not proselytize or evangelize, preach, moralize, or act holier than thou.

Wellness is not even pseudoreligious or metaphysical. There are no wellness horoscopes, fortune-tellers, wizards, or magicians, though a few clever illusionists are known to inhabit the professional ranks.

In my view, wellness is just a way of perceiving things, a mindset or philosophy. The phrase "high level wellness," first used by a physician named Halbert L. Dunn in the mid-1950s, is simply a practical set of ideas for pursuing lifelong physical and psychological well-being in accord with one's changing potentials. It entails an ambitious image of normalcy, embracing a standard far greater and more challenging than the moderation of mediocrity seen in society at the present time.

Wellness is essentially a lifestyle that encompasses a set of principles, such as a belief in the value of making thoughtful, disciplined choices with respect to such issues as exercise and nutrition. It entails skills, such as a capacity for managing stress and functioning with a commitment to embracing personal as well as social responsibility. And, not last and surely not least, wellness can and must lead to a lifelong quest for insights and understanding, satisfaction, and excitement for the greatest quest of all, namely, M&P. Making wise decisions about life's meanings and purposes also gives worksite wellness an added dimension well beyond the usual fitness orientation of corporate health promotion.

In summary, wellness offers those who seek to create their own form of a good life (rather than passively hoping it will happen) a broad set of guides for high levels of being. It is a concept for improving the chances for realizing and enjoying exceptional health. It promotes your chances for a satisfying and fulfilling life perceived as meaningful and filled with worthy purposes. For these reasons, M&P must be the central challenge at the core of a wellness lifestyle.

Does this square with your own impressions of the concept? Is it more than a way of tuning in to an unending array of positive health practices, from fitness, nutrition, managing stress, humor, shaping positive environments, seeking harmony and inner peace on through the list of things people do to care for themselves, including seeking M&P?

The last seems key, to me. All the energy devoted to healthy living ultimately seems a way to search for the best ways to have a life that's meaningful and purposeful. Unlike the health care system, which is about sickness and disease treatment and prevention, the search for meaning in a wellness context is about life enhancement. If war is too important to be left to generals, wellness-based interest in M&P seems too important to be left to doctors, philosophers, shamans, high priests, and other experts. It's your life—and thus your business, first and foremost.

THE FUTURE LIES AHEAD

Wellness, then, can be seen as a mindset for advancing your chances for terrific physical fitness and psychological health. What changes might we see in the key principles, dimensions, and characteristics of the concept—and the movement that grows up around it in medicine and business, if MOL-related matters are given the attention they deserve?

Judd Allen, son of wellness pioneer Robert F. Allen and a leader in his own right, noted at a National Wellness Conference that wellness is starting to encompass "four key themes which cut across the movement, clarify our vision and provide a framework" for nearly everything that follows. He described these as: (1) healthy fun; (2) self-responsibility; (3) mutual respect; and (4) full potential. Seems consistent with the M&P theme, don't you think?

If a key to well-being and meaning is a mindset that advances your chances for terrific physical fitness and psychological health, what beliefs will seem most conducive to such a mindset?

That depends. What it depends on is for you to decide. What do you most care about or need to deal with in order to advance toward terrific physical fitness and psychological health? My assumption throughout this book is that M&P issues lie underneath all else. Lack of exercise, poor nutrition, high stress levels, failure to embrace responsibility, and dreadful health habits from smoking to nail biting are all manifestations of an insufficient sense of who you are, what it's all about, and related existential dysfunctions. The excess weight, risky behaviors, and all the rest are but symptoms of a deeper problem or challenge yet to be adequately addressed. Better to focus on M&P than another diet program, smoking cessation clinic, or other scheme to suppress symptoms.

Check out the possible interest-area options at a wellness conference, in a wellness book, from a wellness speaker, or wherever your desire for learning takes you. Keep it fun and enjoy yourself, find the areas that most excite you and do your best, keeping the big things (family, work, and play) in some kind of balance, most of the time. If you feel creative, see if you are able to express in writing what the idea of a wellness lifestyle means to you. If you do this and like the result, you will be in possession of the only definition that really matters, as far as you're concerned.

Finally, let me end this introductory chapter with a question for you, a riddle, perhaps. What do the Tooth Fairy, Bigfoot, the Loch Ness Monster, and the meaning of life have in common? Give up? Envelope, please (drum roll). The answer is . . . "None of these things exists!" Well, that's my opinion. I think people make them up, for various reasons, for better or worse.

You can get by quite nicely without the Tooth Fairy, Bigfoot, and the Loch Ness Monster but, if you suspect that there's not a single meaning to life applicable to all, you'll want to make up something that's really, well, meaningful to you. Whatever you do, please don't start another religion and add to the amount of myth-information in the world.

NOTES

1. "Why Every Family Needs a Martyr: Not Just for 70 Virgins," *Wall Street Journal,* 15 May 1995, p. 1.

2. Cited in David Friend and the editors of *Life* magazine, *The Meaning of Life* (Boston: Little, Brown & Co., 1991), p. 73.

2

Proposition Two

It Is Better to Reflect on Possibilities Than to Adhere to Dogmas and Creeds.

"This life is a test; it is only a test. If it were a real life, you would receive instructions on where to go, what to believe, and what to do."

Anonymous

INTRODUCTION: A PARTIAL CAVEAT

Hubert Humphrey once remarked, "The right to be heard does not include the right to be taken seriously;" professional basketball player Charles Barkley once quipped that he was misquoted on several occasions in his autobiography! If you are deeply attached to a set of beliefs on any topic, this chapter might really vex you. Sorry about that—please don't take it personally, as some might say. I would add "lighten up," but I know it's not easy maintaining a sense of humor if someone's stomping around on holy ground. Just the same, I respectfully ask that you consider not taking me overly seriously, if you can manage it. After all, if what I write upsets you, I may claim I misquoted myself!

My initial publisher was very concerned that this chapter would be upsetting for some readers. This surprised me— "What's there to be upset about?" was my reaction. This was, of course, due to a faulty self-concept. That's right, you see, I like to think of myself as tolerant and kind, respectful of differences, generous in spirit, lovable, endearing, and so on. Unfortunately, I'm not! But, I'm working at it. Please forgive me if I fall short of my own ideal in this chapter or elsewhere.

Without belaboring this caveat any further, kindly consider that I definitely did *not* write this to vex you, cause premature wrinkling, or otherwise be a pain in the posterior. What follows is just my best thinking about an important element of the quest for meaning and purpose. I *do* reserve the right to change my mind!

SELF-RESPONSIBILITY

I have a problem with any form of dogmatism, defined as an assertion of opinion not to be questioned or reformed, now or evermore, regardless of changes in circumstances or evidence of any kind. This is my problem, I suppose, but since I'm offering a set of principles for facilitating the quest for meaning and purpose as part of wellness living, I need to mention and develop this impression.

One reason for this position on my part is an attachment to the foundation wellness value of self-responsibility. Whatever else this lifestyle or mindset entails, it starts with a conscious embrace of accountability for your own thoughts, attitudes, feelings, deeds, and all the rest. I believe you are more likely to choose and enjoy a continuous quest for added M&P if you remain nondogmatic about your beliefs. Does this seem reasonable to you?

I don't know if your experience was different from mine, but I can't recall any occasions when I was asked to vote on the Ten Commandments. Where I grew up, no teacher gave the impression that these "suggestions" were up for discussion. Not many would expect nuns to do that, I suppose.

A FEW WORDS ABOUT DOGMAS AND CREEDS

It might help to define the terms dogma and creed. According to my dictionary, *dogma* is "a point of view or tenet put forth as authoritative without adequate grounds." It's also "a body of doctrines concerning faith or morals formally stated and authoritatively proclaimed by a church." *Creed* is "a brief authoritative formula of religious belief."

My orientation against dogmas and creeds (D&Cs) developed slowly over time—I can't recall any one thing that turned me into a bit of a rebel. It's all rather odd, in a way, in that I was exposed to little but D&Cs during my first eighteen years in the parochial school system of Philadelphia. On the other hand, this might explain it!

I'll summarize the reasons why I want to encourage you to continually reflect on the nature of life's meaning and purpose and resist the wholesale embrace of D&Cs. It comes back once more to self-responsibility, which makes wellness such an attractive concept. This mindset entails an independent and critical look at data, evidence, information, and input of all kinds. Critical thinking is seen as critical to a healthful, challenging, and satisfying life worthy of your potentials. Qualities of a person devoted to personal responsibility in life seem to include the following:

- confidence in your capacity for sound reasoning;

- an ethical outlook verifiable by experience;

- a healthy respect for the arts and science;

- a healthy skepticism about New Age/Eastern/metaphysical and/or alleged "ancient" and other systems of truths, prophesies, and so on;

- a fondness for finding solutions to human problems in this lifetime;

- a conviction that striving for improvements in the human condition for mankind in general, and individuals specifically, is a source of deep meaning and purpose; and

- an abiding respect for the scientific method as a measure of claims to authority, to knowledge, and to varied degrees of status or credibility.

Does this seem reasonable so far? If these ideas are similar to your own notions about responsibility for beliefs, you probably feel as I do that human affairs are just that—human affairs—not gameboards or battlefields of the gods. Most religions are grounded in D&Cs at odds with this perspective. You simply have to think about the issues and make a choice. My choice is to avoid prepackaged systems for thinking about the most important questions and answers affecting our life on earth. If you feel otherwise, well, I respect that, because as others have said

long before I got here, "*De gustibus non disputandum est.*" (I'm
told that means "about matters of taste, there can be no dis-
pute." Of course, someone could be having me on. For all the
Latin I know, it could mean, "You are a potato head and if your
I.Q. falls any lower, we'll have to water you twice a day.")

So, one of my outrageous ideas that I put to your assessment
is that a safeguard against loss of personal responsibility to the
alleged hazards of D&Cs is to simply reject out-of-hand the entire idea of supernatural interference in human affairs. Personally, I'm convinced that no wizard, no extraterrestrial, and
no "higher power" of any kind has, does, or ever will exist to
meddle in my affairs or anyone else's! For that matter, I don't
think any "lower" power (as in "the devil made me do it!") has
meddled, either. It's worth noting that even many theologians
oppose the idea of an interventionist god who plays a role in
human events, for this would mean the god is capricious and
unpredictable, if not heartless and cruel. (How could we worship a god who occasionally grants field goals but permits
human [and animal] suffering on a global scale?)

Prayer can be an exercise in reckless self-indulgence, favor-
seeking at the expense of others. I'm on many list-servers
wherein e-mail messages sent to a central location are automati-
cally transferred to everyone on the list. A few months ago during hurricane season, someone on a "spirituality" list sent a message "to all Higher Power, prayer/meditation-oriented spirits"
requesting hurricane redirection via meditation and prayer. Reference was made to use of "nonlocal quantum forces" able to
deter dire events. (No, I have no idea what "nonlocal quantum
forces" means.) Meditations and prayers were invited which
would "focus rays of bright thinking on the West Indies and those
in the path of hurricane Marilyn," which was (correctly) pre-
dicted to hit St. Croix and this person's interests located there.

As comedic columnist Dave Barry might say, I'm not making this up. In response, I sent a message to the group as follows:

Dear believers in prayer and meditation about to focus rays of bright thinking on the West Indies and those in the path of Hurricane Marilyn—beware! If you succeed in redirecting Marilyn, be mindful that it has to go somewhere. Maybe you should first get out your maps and include directions as to where (in hell?) it ought to go, so as not to destroy the property and the lives of equally deserving folks who might live in the path of your redirected hurricane. Too bad for them they don't have [the sender of the original e-mail message] praying and meditating for them, but that's not a valid basis for us to visit devastation upon them.

Personally, I don't think that this life will ever be a heaven on Earth and I don't think there's a heaven beyond the earth, either, though the universe is vast beyond comprehension and we could get into a lot of semantic difficulties discussing this. But, I think you know what I mean. I don't believe in hell, either, which means I don't have any devils to deal with or worry about. It's a trade off, I guess.

As far as I see it, you're better off doing what you can to improve the lot of your brothers and sisters while you and they are with us, with an emphasis on keeping your own house in order. Naturally, an important part of doing so is fashioning a wellness lifestyle grounded in an ethic of responsibility; another part is reflecting on your remarkable good fortune to have such a rich vein of M&P possibilities.

FAITH, HOPE, AND CHARITY

It would seem, at first, that only an ogre would take issue with certain revered concepts in our society, such as faith, hope, and charity. Well, I don't want to pick a fight with hope and charity but I think a second opinion is in order regarding the merits of faith. I mention this because faith is the framework supporting D&Cs and thus has to be addressed. Personally, I lost faith in faith a long time ago, particularly in regard to D&Cs.

Consider the possibility that faith is something of a Pandora's box. Open this lid and trouble can follow. I'm sure you are acquainted with the phrase "blind faith," right? While faith can undoubtedly be helpful at times for purposes of comfort, there is little question but that all manner of scary scenes have been loosed upon the planet under its banner. If you doubt it, think of recent events starring faith advocates run amok, including the Reverends Jim Jones and David Koresh, Sheik Abduhl Rahman (who was convicted in October 1995 of planning the World Trade Center bombing), Israeli assassin Yigal Amir, and His Holiness Shoko Asahara (alleged mastermind of the March 1995 Tokyo subway gassing). I'll pass on the temptation to provide a summary of details—I suspect you quite aware of the historical record in this regard. But, it's important to note, all of these people and unnamed others perpetrated their misdeeds (in several cases, murders) in the name of a faith.

D&Cs are founded and sustained by uncritical acceptance and adherence. Of course, this is rather obvious—that why it's called "faith." The lack of independent, critical assessment is the dangerous part of all this. For purposes of seeking meaning and purpose as part of optimal well-being and life satisfaction, how can it ever be desirable to delegate reason to dogma or creed? I'll have to confess—I just don't get it.

In my opinion, many D&Cs promoted as absolute or even sacred truths simply don't ring that way. There is a supermarket of varieties of D&Cs whose advocates claim are God's autobiography. Yet, there are huge conflicts in D&Cs heralded in New Delhi, for instance, with those in Tehran, Jerusalem, and Rome. Even within these locations, there are striking differences in available D&Cs. Unless there is some major flaw in this reasoning, you have to conclude that either all D&Cs are wrong or, at best, only one is right! If the latter, which one? How can we know, if the appeal is to faith?

A belief in faith and attendant D&Cs has nothing to do with intelligence and everything to do with culture, conditioning, and other myriad factors, some only little understood. In many cultures, the majority of people have little freedom to reassess what was ingrained while they were children. In America and most other Western countries, we take freedom of speech for granted. But throughout the world today (and far more so in the past), there are few opportunities to question the predominant or sole "reality" to which humans are or were exposed. If you have the good fortune to be living in a democratic, tolerant, and open society, make the most of your choices by exercising your right to critical judgment.

In thinking about D&Cs, I can't suppress a tendency to wonder if there is not something unhealthy in training children to take information, especially vital information of the highest consequence, on faith. Does this support or encourage their ability to think critically? If it allows parents to convince children to honor and glorify beliefs that fly in the face of science, are they not similarly vulnerable to cultists and other exploiters as the years go by? Personally, I think children should be encouraged to rely on the evidence of their developed senses and encouraged to cultivate reasoning skills.

Obviously, some situations call for skills beyond what may have developed, such as with very young children. A six-year-old has enough to deal with without having to undergo a scaled-back logic lesson concerning why a hot stove should be avoided. "No" or "Stop that right now" will suffice at this stage. Older children or other situations, however, can easily facilitate logical, critical thought. What do you think? Am I on track, or am I overlooking something? Is there value in giving kids faith in Santa Claus, goblins, tooth fairies, and, yes, D&Cs?

It may be that there is a descending scale of reliability in any decision process. At the top of the reliability scale might be logic, then reason, confidence, trust, chance, obedience, hope, and last, and least reliable, faith. If someone argues that everyone goes on faith to some degree and suggests, for example, that getting on an airplane requires it, politely disagree. Explain that boarding a plane can be done with some confidence because the track record of commercial flight provides sufficient *evidence* for safety. This seems more reliable than a hopeful assumption of faith. Into absolutely every decision goes at least one assumption (usually many more). Assumptions are notoriously unreliable. You may have heard the old joke about the word "assume," which is derived from a process which makes an "ass" of "u" and "me."

LEVELS OF RELIABILITY

Assumptions are unavoidable. For example, into every decision about a course of action you intend to pursue is an assumption that you will be alive to pursue it. Formal logic is a process wherein diligent efforts are made to state assumptions explicitly, as premises. This is rarely done in the "real world"; most assumptions are unstated or implicit. No problem here— to do otherwise would make everyday decision-making laborious and time-consuming. It would be akin to a Russian bureaucracy out of control. But, some level of logic can and should be applied to matters of great consequence.[1] The issues associated with all religions seem good candidates for a bit of the rigor which logical reasoning invites.

Another level of reliability is to be expected from sensory awareness. Sensory input is ordinarily reliable but can be defeated, as in optical illusions, among other methods. Sometimes this is unintentional, as with certain natural phenomena. (Recall classic cases of a "mirage" of water bodies appearing in deserts when travellers are experiencing the effects of heat stroke and other forms of dehydration; at other times, it's quite intentional. (I'm thinking here of tent revivals led by Elmer Gantry-style preachers.)

Going down the scale a bit, we find personal testimony as a not-so-reliable technique. Personal testimony is well regarded but shouldn't be! Students taking an evidence class in one of our nation's leading law schools are given a dramatic example of why not. Shortly after starting time for one class early in the semester, a staged fracas breaks out in the front of the classroom. A shouting match degenerates into shoving and one student pulls out a gun, shoots the other, and flees. The professor then asks everyone to take out pen and paper and, without consulting anyone else, write as accurate a description as possible of what just occurred. The descriptions vary wildly. None is complete; only a few come close to accuracy. One factor all accounts have in common is that all of the students seem absolutely sure that their description is flawless. "After all, I'm an eyewitness, aren't I?" to which the professor must reply, "Yes, and your testimony—like that of every other eyewitness you will encounter in the practice of law, is colored by your expectations and memories." Think of this the next time you hear a religious fundamentalist argue that the Bible, a document based on eyewitnesses' stories passed along orally over the course of many generations, is the literal, word-for-word truth.

I think we should be diligent, rigorous, and as explicit as possible in using assumptions, sensory input, and personal testimony to assess D&Cs. What else is there left to use, though? How about logic and reason? Both are a lot more reliable that faith, unstated assumptions, sensory input, and personal testimony. Both are standards used in law. How well would elements of D&Cs stand up to the rigors of logic and reason? Even the faithful would shy from such attempts, arguing that neither logic or reason is appropriate in the context of divine revelation—or whatever. What else? Well, how about a feeling of confidence in one thing or another? Confidence is high on the reliability chain. We may be confident of something on the basis of its track record or the history of similar situations, without taking the time to examine the particulars of the current situation. "My car started last winter when it was fifteen degrees below zero, so I'm confident it will do so again this year." We overtly recognize that there are varying levels of confidence: "My car started last winter when it was fifteen below zero and I'm pretty sure it will do so now that it's thirty below—but I'm not willing to bet the farm on it."

What else? Trust! Trust is similar to confidence except that, due to the way language has evolved, we usually express confidence in things and trust in people. (However, a good rule of thumb is never trust anyone who says "Let me be honest with you about this!" Whenever I hear someone say this, I always wonder about the integrity of what he told me prior to this remark.) Trust is often placed in people who don't necessarily have a track record of good decisions. Thus, I'd rate it lower on the scale of reliability than confidence—especially when faced with financial appeals from television ministries! The track record, in this case, is (to put it kindly) suspect.

Chance? Not so reliable! The roll of the dice, the flip of the coin, the turn of the card—seems like a hell of a way to make up your mind, doesn't it? Yet, how else do people choose a denomination and the D&Cs that go with it? Chance. The chance of convenient location, prominence of the minister, friends who did the recruiting, and so on seem to play the dominant roles in choices by chance. However, in real-world terms, you can do worse! Reasonable people probably do not resort to chance as a decision-making technique unless they have reduced the alternatives to two or three options, none of which is clearly better than any of the others. In short, your time is probably better spent going with chance (instinct?) at this point than in dithering over exactly which of a few choices will give you that extra one percent of benefit. At least the concept of chance implies the choice between alternatives, which means you haven't just blindly accepted the first idea that popped into your head. And, of course, chance has a real role to play in experimentation, where you want to be sure that the choices of, say, which patients get real drugs and which get placebos, isn't governed by hidden assumptions or prejudices.

How about obedience? Not good at all for purposes of reliability, but it seems to work well for the pope. Obedience can be a corrupted form of trust, even when the intent is benign. The implication here is that you are doing what someone else tells you to do, but for reasons of pressure, coercion, immaturity, feelings of inadequacy, sacred obligation, threat, etc.—not a free-will decision.

I can't overlook hope! Hope can be right at the edge of unconscious thought as well as near the bottom of the reliability ladder. If I were to say "My car started last winter when it was fifteen below zero and I think it will do so now that it's sixty below," I've passed out of the realm of confidence and into the domain of wishful thinking, or, in a word, hope. Pop psychology has a buzzword for hope when it replaces acceptance of reality or constructive action: denial! We see this a lot today in the promotion of bogus remedies for "cures" when there is little prospect of recovery and nothing but "hoping" for a miracle remains. Many unscrupulous entrepreneurs sell junk as complementary byproducts of hopeless hope. As Jack Raso* has observed, alternative health care gets a lot of mileage from hope, particularly in the forms of mysticism and the supernatural. The former is a belief in "realities accessible only through subjective experience"; the latter is "belief in entities, or forces, that are outside of, yet affect, the universe." Referring back to denial, this is a process of decision-making when the evidence points toward a conclusion that you really don't want to deal with (e.g., that your illness is irreversible), so decisions are made in the hope that what you want will come true.

And, as has been noted, there is faith at the bottom of the hierarchy of reliable "thought" processes. This is, in my view, the decision-making tool of last resort and the one most favored by the promoters of D&C. If there were any evidence at all to support a conclusion, if there were any more reliable decision-making technique available, the promoters of D&Cs would still use faith. Heck, why not—I would if I had a dogma

---

*Jack Raso is co-editor of *Nutrition Forum* and author of *Alternative Healthcare,* the most comprehensive guide to nonestablished treatments available (Amherst, N.Y.: Prometheus Books, 1994).

I wanted to advance, as in, "Why no, there is no evidence for my dogma—you just have to take it on faith." Saves a lot of energy, for one thing. Faith is there to support conclusions for which there is no credible evidence and no logical basis for the truth, validity, efficacy, or efficiency of D&Cs. That's the way faith works. It is, as noted, applied when there's little reason for believing or doing what faith would lead you to do. Recognizing this, advocates of faith in general and attendant D&Cs in particular spend a lot of time, energy, and effort extolling the virtues of this least reliable decision-making tool.

Corinthians 13:2 suggests that "faith can move mountains" but omits mention of the specific mountain that gave rise to this aphorism. "Have faith" and "keep the faith, baby," are common catch-phrases, but I personally prefer "Keep the baby, Faith." Religionists of all denominations regularly praise faith. This recalls a well understood persuasion technique called "the big lie." Say something over and over, shout it from the rooftops, make songs about it, praise it fulsomely at every turn, and pretty soon everybody will take it for granted, as part of the cultural background, without ever questioning it.

I think you have to be just a bit gullible to take "on faith" a belief system upon which you base a significant part of your life. Shortly after finishing the first draft of this book, I had a meeting with the top editors of the company that had paid an advance on the work. One editor, speaking for the other, expressed great concern about this chapter being offensive to many of their regular readers. Then she added, "Reading this chapter made me feel so stupid." I was, of course, too polite to say so, but I have to confess to wondering at the time, "Well, then, why persist in thinking in a fashion that, upon reflection, makes you feel this way?"

These are a few of my sentiments in support of the proposition that you are better off not allowing dogma or creed to affect (inhibit) your quest for meaning and purpose. The case for or advantage of doing so seems nonexistent to me, but that's just my perspective. Let's move on to see what other perspectives were offered by the wellness promoters and practitioners I asked to comment on this idea.

COMMENTS BY WELLNESS PROMOTERS

It was hard to find many wellness promoters who defended D&Cs. Even those who objected to the first proposition said they agreed with me on this one. Francie M. Berg, who actually had something good to say about D&Cs, believes that a religious dogma or creed can provide some people with a firm foundation or structure. Problems arise, however, because D&Cs are rigid and limiting. Still, there are people for whom a religious upbringing based on D&Cs gives certain roots.

Sandra Martin agreed, but reluctantly, stating that "it's unfortunate that proposition number two is true. Faith is a process of growth that is often hindered by D&C."

Thomas R. Collingwood of Richardson, Texas is one of the strongest defenders of D&Cs who responded to this proposition:

> Many of the problems we are experiencing in our society, especially among youth, are due to a lack of any D&Cs. We need the basic structure of a creed to serve as a platform for interpreting our experience and for giving direction to our efforts. It is not just a religious matter. The scientific method is a good example. A theory or construct must be made "a priori" in order to make any meaning of data. Relativism has,

unfortunately, become the creed in our society and a source for many problems. To be fully functioning and responsible individuals we need a greater emphasis on time-honored creeds (such as many religions profess). Only with a stable and disciplined frame of reference can we, as individuals, be "free" to grow and pursue all our possibilities.

Steven Jonas of Stonybrook, New York expressed a view more in line with my own:

> Religion can be both mind-expanding and mind-imprisoning. To the extent it relies on faith and self-exploration of the relationship between self and God, it is mind-expanding. To the extent it relies on dogma, rules, regulations, and quotes from given sources of "what's right," it is mind-imprisoning. In general, the further religious experience is separated from organized religion, the more liberating it will be. The more any organized religion attempts to use the law to enforce its worldview on everyone, the more imprisoning it is, for believers and nonbelievers alike.

Steven also suggested that D&Cs were a danger to freedom: "To me, the MOL or an LOM [life of meaning] in America at this time is to defend freedom and democracy in the face of attempted restrictions by forces of the religious right. Freedom is crucial to wellness. It must not be curtailed if we are to be well."

Carol Garzona, a zen-oriented wellness writer, offered this somewhat mystical thought:

> Religious D&Cs often have the effect of discouraging openness to discovery. . . . They tend to dictate one way and only this way when there are many ways, and some ways are easier

and better for different people. . . . But there is a way for everyone. . . . Again, we not only have to discover "The Meaning," we also have to discover "The Way" to the Meaning. The goal is to merge into/become the Meaning.

Jay Eacker urged an appreciation of the complexities in the matter:

Religious D&Cs may very well discourage lifelong openness to life's varied possibilities and desirable meanings but, on the other hand, so may any other meaning we ascribe to life. To hold to any view about the MOL precludes holding any other view and therefore, it is not just religious creeds and doctrines that may discourage such openness. However, religious creeds and doctrines may provide us with a feeling of certainty about the MOL when it is a subject about which certainty is not possible.

What are you thinking at this point? Are D&Cs overly rigid constraints on your own exercise of responsibility in the choice of value systems? Or are they a valid guideposts most of the time? How can children or less educated folks be supported in discerning positive from destructive D&Cs? Who can make the decision about what is positive versus what's destructive? Doesn't it seem hopelessly complicated, sometimes? Maybe that's the biggest advantage and source of the popularity of D&Cs—you don't have to think so much and be so darned responsible for everything!

This might make Deb Jones's succinct commentary on this proposition seem mighty attractive. Deb read the proposition and responded: "Hear, hear!" If only all my readers and audience members were this responsive and supportive!

Tim Madigan, the editor of the Buffalo, New York-based *Free Inquiry* magazine, sees humor as key to strengthening your immune system against the perils of blind belief and other hazards of D&Cs:

Steve Allen, in the introduction to his book *Funny People,* writes: "Without laughter, life on our planet would be intolerable." I heartily concur. Humor is essential to our wellbeing. We live in a world with many problems, both natural and manmade. What laughter at its best does is to put things in perspective. It helps to bring down the walls of intolerance and causes us to reexamine our doctrinaire positions. We wish to understand the world we find ourselves in, which means that no subject should be off-limits. Why did the chicken cross the road? Irreverence opens up new areas to explore, by getting beyond a sense of awe which can impede critical thinking. When the righteous ask: "Is nothing sacred?" I reply "Why are you so concerned about nothing?" How much better it would have been if Abraham slapped his knee and chortled: "You want me to do *what* to my first-born son? What a sense of humor you've got, Big Guy!" Friedrich Nietzsche once wrote: "I would believe only in a god who could dance." I would amend that to "I would believe only in a god who could take a joke." It is the people whose hearts have been hardened by certainty who find it most difficult to let loose and guffaw. They are unwilling to challenge their own convictions, and they detest anyone who pokes fun at their beliefs. We should be ever mindful of the importance of humor as a self-corrective method of keeping us from becoming stern absolutists. In the words of that great philosopher Henny Youngman, "Take my creed, please!"

Maryann Rapposelli of Newark, Delaware sees fear, not curiosity about or an interest in a search for meaning, coming from D&Cs. However, Maryann has an antidote— play!

> Imagine if we did not undermine our happiness by allowing ourselves to succumb to the unjustified fears that infiltrate our risk-taking and decision-making. Think of it: Why are children so happy and carefree? Because they are consumed by play, which is devoid of fear. We are most truly ourselves when at play. Strive to express yourself through play or playful thoughts, whether at work (especially at work), home, or at leisure. Let play pervade life. Strive not to be consumed by religious creed or dogma-based fear, which the religious right is expert at doing to people. If under attack by creed or dogma, try a sure-fire remedy—play.

Jenna Scott of Temple, Texas, had this to say about independent reflection versus dogma: "There were years in my life filled with religious dogma. There were years when my own life was meaningless because I was too busy taking care of other people. The discovery of M&P came late. I say float your own boat, or paddle your own canoe, so to speak."

Well, I want to shift this commentary to a few suggestions that might help you promote M&P with others, whatever your opinion on the D&C matter, but first, I have a treat for you. My darling daughter Jeanne, living in Mill Valley, California, takes a view of D&Cs that might be of interest to anyone not quite so adamant about this proposition as I am. Maybe you will enjoy Jeanne's remarks:

> We all need to find a form of M&P that works for us: I believe we humans are not capable of grasping the reality of eternally mystifying questions regarding the existence (or absence) of

God and mankind's ultimate purpose on Earth. So, I'm not even going to try. All those religious zealots who think they "know" the ultimate truth because "it is written" are being fooled but, if it makes them feel better about themselves, answers questions and makes their world less full of chaos . . . , then whatever. As for me, what it's all about, since we can't know anything about what will happen after death or what we should be doing, etc., is just to enjoy life as much as possible this time around. "Enjoy the passage of time," is the way I heard someone put it. And for me, this means fulfilling, close relationships with you, Mom, [dear brother] Jon, and my circle of friends; . . . amusing myself; appreciating all the blessings I've been so lucky to have; being thankful for lack of tragedy, for health, for all my great experiences, happiness, humor, everyday joys and positive feelings and living in accordance with my own values. (. . . You know, being generally nice to people and creatures, honesty, generosity, and helpfulness whenever possible. These are good values, I think.)

So, that's about it, not something that will win any Nobel Prize or anything but, hey, it works for me.

It works for me, too, so maybe I'll start a religion and make it the basis for a new set of D&Cs!

WHAT TO MAKE OF IT ALL

I suspect that fear of dogma-defenders has discouraged the introduction of M&P as a wellness issue in corporate and educational settings. What sensible wellness promoter would want risk setting off a brouhaha by stimulating a discussion that some creed-attached person might and surely would find offensive or inappropriate or otherwise upsetting? Is there any way to avoid this? Do you think there are ways to discuss the importance of M&P as part of a healthy lifestyle without offending sensibilities? If not, should we accept the fact that some may choose to become offended, but that the topic of M&P is too important to be avoided for this reason? Can those who facilitate M&P discussions be protected? Perhaps a little controversy can be managed, with skilled leadership and guidance of discussions and negotiations. Let's explore this a bit.

My good friend Robert F. Allen, a pioneer in advancing wellness at work and school sites, tried hard to put values at the forefront of wellness discussions. He knew the term spirituality was fraught with difficulties, but thought that ways could be found to manage them.

Bob talked a lot about wellness near the end of life, or at any time when difficulties seemed to overwhelm the seeker of well-being. In doing so, Bob changed the orientation that physical health had to be the predominant measure of well-being. Bob and others who shared this awareness brought an alternative way of seeing things to the attention of health promoters, myself included.

A key lesson that came from Bob's work in values promotion was the idea that, in sickness and in health, we can choose how to perceive a situation. Just as one can experience wellness in the midst of any disease or disability, so can a range of M&P options be tolerated, if one chooses to take this perspective. This lesson can apply to our concern about the flexibility of those deeply wedded to D&Cs. What a gift if you, the wellness promoter, parent, or friend, can persuade an enthusiast for any belief or nonbelief system to allow diversity to take its course in this respect. Let's examine for a minute the case for discussing M&P as a way of discussing D&Cs without rancor or other negative effects and why it is so valuable to do so.

Consider, for starters, that most managers would not expect high performance from employees with severe emotional disturbances, warped minds, bizarre beliefs, weird attitudes, or crazy habits. Having an entire organization of such folks would probably be unhealthy, as well as unprofitable. Yet, if your people are expected to go about their duties and otherwise conduct their lives with few useable clues about their overall purposes or even hypotheses about what they are doing on the planet, besides surviving, there might be cause for concern! Such a situation would, in fact, be hazardous to well-being of the organization, not to mention the life, liberty, and the pursuit of even a minimal level of happiness of the employees. Yet, there could be elements of this condition in your organization.

Psychiatrist Irvin Yalow in *Existential Psychotherapy** claimed that there is professional consensus for the idea that "the majority of patients are bedeviled by a lack of meaning in their lives." A "bedeviled mind" is clearly not a good thing or a healthy quality. Functioning in this fashion interferes with achieving and maintaining a high level of performance. And, what if these patients, those without meaning, are the healthy ones? After all, they have either had the good sense to seek professional help for their existential anxieties or the good fortune to be institutionalized for behaviors caused by their absence—the rest of us could be toughing it out while adrift in meaninglessness. In either case, the situation can be improved and a dialogue can be initiated. To overcome the discomfort of discussing D&Cs in a M&P context, a safe environment is needed. If you want to create such a setting, you need to know the obstacles to open, democratic discussions where tolerance is the watchword. Here are

---

*(New York: Basic Books, 1980). See chapter 11, "Meaninglessness and Psychotherapy," pp. 461–83.

a few ideas and tips for moving ahead, helping people examine their D&Cs as a way of finding added M&P.

Try to remember that D&Cs have been learned, followed, and ingrained over many years, usually without any question, so people unconsciously feel defensive about such deep-seated beliefs. Such learning patterns sometimes make an openness to objective appraisals seem wrong or sinful, which hardly encourages dialogue. Instead, defenses are evoked. In such cases, D&Cs must be addressed indirectly, by focusing on other possible meaning systems. Treading on D&Cs can be like walking on a booby trap, and misplaced efforts to stimulate critical thinking might get you blown up!

I recall as a child being told that three topics were to be avoided in polite company (and impolite company should be avoided anyway). The three were politics, sex, and religion. As the years passed, politics and sex came off the list. (In fact, dealing with these issues sometimes made me the life of the party!) Religion, and varied D&Cs that are part of religions, stayed on the forbidden list much longer, until my college years, when it replaced politics and sex as the best of all topics for worthwhile discussions! But, the point is, dealing with D&Cs was at first discouraged and initially quite difficult. Don't expect that it will be easy to do from the start.

Why do you suppose directors of corporate health promotion and others responsible for varied forms of wellness programming avoid religion and, at most, refer to the vaguer word "spirituality?" I think it's because of discomfort and intimidation. I think it's because they fear controversy related to D&Cs. Of course, it is true that conflicting religious beliefs often generate discord, confusion, and anxiety—or worse, as witness the battles that rage around such matters as maintaining a separation of church and state, abortion, and related issues. Furthermore, nearly all religions profess to teach their own "truths" about why we're here and what this life is all about (most favor another one redeemable after death). Thus, to hold a forum or otherwise orchestrate a symphony of ideas about spirituality is seen as an invitation for "trouble." Too many believers have an unfortunate tendency to defend what they have learned from religious leaders over a period of decades. If socialized to this extent, most will find the idea of bringing such teachings into question, even indirectly via discussions of M&P, uncomfortable and intimidating. The result is that consultants and educators perceive controversy, anger, and other forms of wellness education that might upset constituents as bad for business and therefore a consummation devotedly to be avoided, and who can fault them for this?

A partial solution to this problem might lie in the fact that people of all educations, religious beliefs, and other categories want to have meaningful discussions about their purposes, whatever their D&Cs, if any. By insisting upon and reinforcing an attitude of acceptance for all D&Cs, faiths, beliefs, religions, myths, and the rest, worksite dialogues on the spiritual aspect of well-being can be managed successfully. The same applies to discussions among friends. In both cases, we should worry less that a variety of different D&Cs will unleash a new series of religious crusades. People are a lot more open than many wellness promoters realize (myself included).

Yes, it can be done—and you can do it if you are willing to be just a bit of a risk-taker! To facilitate things without fear of unleashing bloody carnage, you could start out with a simple survey. Make up a questionnaire that will appeal to the rational as well as orthodox types. The goal is simply to generate interest in M&P concerns.

One proven way to get people in the mood for a M&P discussion is to present a few ideas expressed by others—and ask for comments. You can use examples listed in the bibliography at the end of this book or even ideas from the wellness leaders and practitioners quoted throughout.

The main goal is an interesting, anger-free discussion. People are often surprised to discover the extent of variation in perspectives they and their friends/associates have on M&P. The same may be true of D&Cs.

Consider offering a value inventory to spark comments. Here's one you can adapt to suit your tastes. Since I wrote this one, it might be a bit more provocative than you may prefer. If so, tone it down a bit. On the other hand, you might think I'm an M&P wuss, so fire it up! Do whatever you like.

- Would you like to explore the "spiritual" aspect of the body/mind/spirit, without having things get vaguely "spiritual?"

- Are you ever frustrated by appeals to faith? What alternatives might you prefer?

- Does anything about the D&Cs of your youth tend to make you feel guilty or uneasy?

- Would you welcome more opportunities to discuss M&P as a health issue or in any other context?

- Have you doubts about the existence of God, or gods? Do you feel comfortable discussing these doubts with others? Do you ever wonder if there's something wrong with you for doubting when so many seem convinced?

- Do you think there are connections between what people see as their purpose in life and how they live, including their lifestyle commitments and practices?

- Are your beliefs different from your parents and many of your friends and associates, and is this important in any way?

- Do you think D&Cs sometimes substitute for other needs?

- Can morality be expected from persons without a religious faith? Is a secular person as likely to be ethical?

- Can this life have meaning and purpose if you do not hold a belief in a life after death?

Persons who respond "Yes" to these questions are likely to welcome discussions or other explorations of D&Cs. They are good candidates to share ideas with others. Life really is uncertain and it is not enough to "eat dessert first" as a means for dealing with it. In everyday, practical ways, life proves itself not just uncertain but scary as hell.

The trick or key is to change this situation, to end the neglect of M&P in wellness programming. Bringing into the light of quiet discussion dogmas and creeds that otherwise close people to a tolerance for diversity, openness to ideas, and sympathy for belief systems different from their own can be a liberating act.

If you explore ways to deal with inhibiting D&Cs as a wellness promoter, you will surely find that the field has become more interesting and significant. Many existing corporate programs simply borrow the term wellness because it's a popular buzzword. Most corporate wellness programs are, in fact, simply risk management, illness-avoidance, traditional health education endeavors that operate on the old medical model. This means doctors and nurses remain the experts, the ultimate authorities on what makes for "health." Partial results of this paradigm are boring rules and tests, a focus on the body, and a barrier to communicating the fact that responsibility for health and life quality rests with the individual, not the experts. A related result of the old system is that the body, not the "soul" of M&P, remains the animus or driving force.

I suspect you would agree that corporate wellness programs need to get people looking beyond their bodies to the mental and emotional dimensions of their being. Isn't this the real bottom line of wellness? The theory here is that if more people can be made aware of and excited about a greater range of meaning and purpose-in-life options, more folks might decide to take better care of their bodies, as part of making more of their existence!

The rhetorical question "Who will benefit most from M&P explorations?" can be answered at last: "Anyone with a belief system adversely affected by D&Cs, for starters. And, of course, others not so burdened, that's who."

And, it could be noted, some who have strong attachments to D&Cs are marvelously well, also. If it works, whatever "it" is and nobody is hurt by it, it can't be all bad. In any event, in free societies, we ought to not only be allowed to discuss these issues but feel comfortable in doing so.

THE FUTURE LIES AHEAD

Reflections on M&P free of all or even most D&Cs will, in my view, promote more fulfilling, affirmative views of existence. The latter can entail positive images and values, such as freedom, happiness, fulfillment, love, and moral responsibility to others—and that's just a beginning! All these qualities can be moved to the top of the wellness list of outcome goals, and compare favorably with most D&Cs, for a lot of people.

How does this resonate with you? Do you think this proposition is an appropriate topic for corporate wellness, on a par with body composition, target heart rates, and a balanced diet with lots of fiber and eight glasses of water daily? If not, why not? How else can we get there? What do we believe? Most of us, I think, know that health is not an end in itself but an asset for the rest, including those vaunted M&P aspects that make life worthwhile, at least for those fortunate enough to recognize them.

What are the implications of this proposition for M&P and promoting wellness at the workplace and in educational settings? One consequence might be to render the medical model less dominant. If the agenda shifted from risk reduction and physical fitness to freedom, human happiness, fulfillment, love, and moral responsibility to others, to note but a few possibilities, we would indeed have greater public interest in wellness! Perhaps a healthier population might follow.

Of course, it is important to remember that life is complex. Intervene at one point and things change all down the line. If, for instance, M&P becomes the focus of wellness programming at the corporate and other levels, a danger far greater than nurse and doctor domination might present itself. Can you guess what that mortal perdition might be? Clergy domination! Suppose the wellness advocates of the year 2000 were to promote not discussions of M&P issues for your determination based on your free will, life experience, judgement, respect for science, and so on, but rather their ideas about what constitutes *the* meaning of life—and more D&Cs! (And why am I thinking of the pharisees, Martin Luther, and Christian fundamentalists at this moment?)

To me, this would be an abomination. Who wants ayatollahs, high priests, and other champions of every imaginable D&C promoting wellness? This would be a very different situation from what we know today. It might make many of us long for the old days of the medical model controlled by doctors focused on illness, risks, and the rules for physical health.

Well, it's something to think about. Meanwhile, ask yourself if you think the people of America, Australia, Canada, and other nations are ready for M&P dialogues free of D&C domination.

Perhaps a better question for wellness promoters might be: How can anyone justify *not* making M&P questions (as opposed to meaning of life answers) a vital element in wellness education?

NOTE

1. Two excellent resources for appreciating levels of reliability are *Dumbth,* by Steve Allen (Amherst, N.Y.: Prometheus Books, 1991), and *Easily Fooled,* by Robert Fellows (Minneapolis: Mind Matters, Inc., 1992).

3

Proposition Three

Most People Now, as in the Past, Live Lives That Are Nasty, Brutal, Meaningless, and Short; Life Need Not Be Nasty, Brutal, or Meaningless. It Will Still Be Short.

"More than at any time in history, mankind faces a crossroads. One road leads to despair and utter hopelessness; the other to annihilation and ruin. Let us pray we have the wisdom to choose wisely."

Woody Allen

Life is short. I would have been surprised if any wellness leader or practitioner, or anyone else for that matter, quarreled with the last part of this lengthy assertion, namely, that life is short. None did, and it is unlikely you would, either. Let's face it, the presence of human life (versus 3.5 billion years of other life forms) on this good 4.6-billion-year-old planet does not suggest that we are exactly dominant.[1] Our species (*Homo sapiens*) goes back about 250,000 years; our earliest ancestor (*Australopithecus afarensis*) first appeared less than four million years ago. To put things in perspective, consider Mark Twain's analogy. In his day, the Eiffel Tower was the world's tallest building. Twain noted the age of the universe (as accepted at that time) versus the brief period of human existence, then ("tongue-in-cheek") observed that the planet must have been created for our benefit:

> If the Eiffel Tower were now representing the world's age, the skin of paint on the pinnacle knob at its summit would represent man's share of that age; and anybody would perceive that the skin was what the Tower was built for. I reckon they would. I dunno.[2]

Stephen Jay Gould updates Twain's analogy by noting that human existence occupies but "the last geological millimicrosecond of this history—the last inch of the cosmic mile . . ." and urges us to "accept the implications and learn to seek the meaning of human life . . . with joy in the challenge if our temperament be optimistic."[3]

Life is nasty, brutal, and meaningless. On this part of the proposition, I expected an argument—and was not disappointed! Of course, many agreed with me, as well. What are your first reactions? I'm sure this depends in good part on how you interpret my statement, and in some measure on your sense of the quality of your own life. Just to be as clear as I can, I simply mean that, based on my own short life's observations, most people throughout human history and even at the present time seem to have enjoyed a lot less political freedom, intellectual opportunity, material comfort, and joy in life than my friends and I have experienced—and most of us are still looking for *more*! In addition, it's my sense that vast numbers of humans have endured lives damaged and/or terminated prematurely by famines, wars, and all manner of cruelty, hardship, and suffering.

Am I mistaken about this, or could I have thought of this proposition as a young child when hearing a few childhood thrillers such as Jack and Jill, Hansel and Gretel, Bambi, Dumbo, and the like? All have themes of abandonment, pain, dismemberment, and death that might have hinted that life could, on occasions, get nasty, brutal, and a bit meaningless. Not to put a dark perspective on things, but you have to admit that those Grimm Brothers were not exactly a thousand laughs!

Whether the proposition is more or less true or not, the implication of the statement is simply that you probably have an opportunity for a pretty good life that will not last anything even remotely like forever, that most other humans have (and have had) a much worse set of conditions with which to survive, cope, or prosper—so make the best of life, while you have it. Which, in my (long) view, won't be long.

Now what do *you* think?

Let's look at a few of the reactions I got.

COMMENTS BY WELLNESS PROMOTERS

Francie M. Berg of Hettinger, North Dakota, was among the first to invoke the old "it depends" caution, which of course is true for nearly every assertion, particularly this one:

> Proposition three depends on who you're talking about. [It does not apply to] most of the people I know, who live in this community and state. I believe we value each person as an individual, probably because we have so few—and we all know we're needed. People have a lot of worries, and many live lives of quiet desperation, but I can't agree their lives are brutal or meaningless. On the other hand, if we're talking world-

wide, where the masses of people may live on the edge of starvation with dying children, struggling with the most basic needs of life, under a harsh government, then, yes, the majority of lives may be short, brutal, and seemingly meaningless.

Doctor Steven Jonas responded: "Life is short only for those who make it so, for 'short' in time encompasses not only the number of days, but what one does with them."

Carol Garzona pointed out that the key variable is something other than material prosperity or impoverishment:

Our lives are "brutal" and "meaningless" only to the degree that we are not on the path to our own discoveries. A person with great luxuries and ease who is not on the path of discovery has a far more "brutal" life than one who has physical miseries but has moved at least one inch on the path of discovery/merging.

Jay Eacker of Walla Walla, Washington seemed less than pleased, and seconded Garzona's point:

This proposition suffers from the same limitations as all the other propositions and proposals about the MOL. We cannot know that other lives are nasty, brutal, meaningless, and short, since it is we who claim to know. Other lives may be pleasant, full of meaning, sublime, and long, depending upon the M&P of life assigned, found, or invented by those who live them.

Jim Ward, a champion triathlete nearing his eighth decade, had this to offer:

To fulfill our goals in life, we have to be fit and full of energy. In the past fifty years, medical science has added twenty years to our lifespan. Life is still short and time flies but, fortunately, improvements in our knowledge of nutrition and physical training enable us to achieve a sense of fitness and physical well-being as we age that our ancestors never enjoyed. Many of us today, with an added lifespan, are able to swim, bike, and run further and faster than anyone our age has ever done before. In the leisure of our retirement, we are feeling fit, having fun, and rising to the challenges of competition in our age groups. That makes life meaningful.

The wellness promoters and practitioners all indicated that life is meaningful when excellence is prized over mediocrity, when the bare survival attitude of trying to cope and get by is replaced with what Karen McFee of Wayne, Pennsylvania, called "life abundant:"

I want to do more than cope. I want to thrive. So, I manage my stress. I want to do more than think. I want to be creative. So, I get enough sleep. I want to do more than make it through the day, I want to be energetic. So, I eat nutritional foods. . . . I want more than acquaintances. I want friends. So, I reach out to others. I want to do more than search for happiness. I want peace. So, I pray. I want to do more than survive. I want to live. So, I laugh and cry. I want more than life. I want life abundant. Then I discover that I want more than life abundant. I want others to have it as well. So, I promote health.

One reason life is brutal as well as short for many people is due to their inability or unwillingness to "seize the day." Instead, they permit others to run their lives. Jenna Scott addressed this point, suggesting that we would all do better to choose our own agenda, including our own means of finding

M&P: "Life is a do-it-yourself project. Think your own thoughts. Feel your own feelings. Choose your own agenda. If you don't, other people will come along and fill your life up with theirs."

Some wellness promoters find great value in consciously reminding themselves of the miracle as well as the brevity of life—and use this knowledge to celebrate the gift aliveness represents. Note the words of Patti Shank of Columbia, Maryland:

> I used to spend a lot of time worrying about dying. I expressed my concerns to a close friend, who helped me to see the awe of my aliveness, even though death is inevitable. The fact that we exist is by itself nothing short of amazing, regardless of how long or short life is. The miracle is having been alive at all! The unlikeliness of being conceived, and once conceived, being ourselves (out of the billions of combinations that might have occurred!) is staggering! Whether we live ten minutes, ten years, or ten decades, our existence is a true miracle, never to be repeated.

Jerry Krause of Spokane, Washington, has a response to this reality that may be an antidote if not a cure for any lingering dismay with our temporal nature:

> The MOL trick is to increase "life expectancy." It's not how long but how well you live. We all need to expect as much as possible from life. A solid foundation for MOL is based on developing potential and retaining capacity to move. Thus, physical fitness (and attendant skills) are truly the hub of the wellness wheel. The fit and skilled person becomes a movement monster who really pays attention to an active wellness lifestyle.

Michael Johnson of Milton, Wisconsin, an HIV-positive educator who travels the nation with his wife teaching assemblies of high school students about AIDS prevention, thinks the mind is key:

> Quantum physics has shown that all matter is composed of quarks, sub-atomic bundles of pure energy. Hence, tangible matter is nothing more than an illusion perpetrated upon us by limited physical senses which are too coarse to perceive reality. Thus, it follows that the mind is not in the body. The body is firmly in the mind.

Barbara D. Braden of Belton, Missouri, sees M&P as a choice, a side order, so to speak:

> Life comes served with a side of cole slaw. Whether it's positive or negative is a matter of perception. I don't happen to prefer cole slaw with sugar (it usually comes that way), but I still try it every time just to make certain I'm not missing something wonderful. It is, after all, what we choose to do with what we are served that brings meaning to our life. Free will, choice—that most precious commodity. Life is communion, the exchange of body, mind, and spirit. It is taking in and giving back, like the waves' ebb and flow. We choose what we take into ourselves through our senses and past our skin.

Laurie A. Kelley's reaction to this proposition reminds us that life is not brutal or meaningless if we connect with others, and goes on to make the case for learning about M&P via relationships:

> A sense of purpose in your life can often be found by following your natural instinct for connecting. As humans, we are blessed with a wonderful desire to seek out relationships, to look for and find special people [who] will acknowledge, rec-

ognize, love, and support us. Even as infants we eagerly awaited our parents' loving gaze, seeking connection through the windows of the soul, our eyes. It is only through relationship that we truly learn who we are. Haven't relationships led you on a path of knowing more clearly what you want, what you do not want, what angers you, what saddens you, what softens you, what brings you joy? With others by our side, we find our courage and our strength, as well as our weakness and grief. Allow yourself to seek out relationships. And look at them thoughtfully, knowing that you are gazing into the mirror that reflects your special journey.

WHAT TO MAKE OF IT ALL

If it's true that most worksite officials, such as school educators and company managers, are uncomfortable with "spirituality" and related terms for addressing M&P issues as discussed in Part One, it probably would not be a good idea to offer a brown bag luncheon entitled, "Wellness: A Cure-All for Your Nasty, Brutal, Meaningless, and Short Life." No, this would not be tactful. What you might want to do is seek to create a mood wherein few will get intimidated or menaced by this or any other proposition, whether it be mine, yours, or someone else's. Make discussions comfortable for diversity—in the sense of ideas different from what everybody holds. Try to get across the notion that all ideas, even the one expressed in this proposition, are understandable, given the varied reinforcement people have had. Note that anyone in the room would be convinced that the moon is made of rice pudding if enough information to bolster and fortify this view—and no others, year after year—was provided. In other words, don't take it personally—nobody is saying *your* particular life is nasty, brutal, meaningless, or short—at least no more so than the norm! And, if someone is, who cares, what does it matter?

The objective, then, is to get as many of your friends and associates as possible to talk about their beliefs, whatever they are.

Maybe this would be a good time for you to express, in a paragraph or so, how you would rewrite this particular proposition! See if you can comfortably make a related statement more attuned to your own ideas, for you and/or most people.

Here's a space where you can do so:

_____

_____

_____

_____

_____

I'm willing to bet that, at least in western societies, most people are a lot more open to explorations about their M&P and to exchanges of ideas on whether life is nasty, brutal, meaningless, and short than you might think. Give it a try—live dangerously. What's the worst that can happen, besides life becoming well, nasty, brutal, meaningless, and short?

THINGS YOU MIGHT TRY WITH OTHERS

As one who makes a living working with students and employees in the area of developing M&P as a career asset, I have discovered that most people love to talk about and explore with each other these kinds of questions. At first, most are not nearly as articulate and comfortable discussing the subject, especially when it is broad-based, like "What is the meaning of life?" That's how I came to write the propositions.

You can assume that, unlike the hundred wellness promoters and practitioners whose comments you can review in these pages, the people you will deal with will not, at first, be bold about sharing their thoughts and ideas about M&P. That's why you want to create a certain kind of atmosphere wherein specific zingers like this proposition are put on the table. Do this and I predict you will discover people have a lot more to offer on this profound topic than you or they first thought.

Just remember, conditions must be right for disclosure. What are the "right" conditions? Well, for starters, it helps if people are given a bit of encouragement, if the environment is safe for whatever notions may be deeply held, if the mood created is conducive to creativity, and if you can add a dash of stimulation to the topic at hand. Fun works wonders, as well. Of course, nobody can tell you exactly how to encourage these and other necessary conditions in your family, school, workplace, or wherever you wish to do a bit of M&P brainstorming, since the variations are limitless.

Still, I want to keep encouraging you to be a brave soul, anyway. Experiment—you'll probably get good at it. I would not be surprised if you were to find that many people not only participate but very much enjoy the process of exploring M&P, from an "as is" to the more important "could be" perspective. And there is no harm in reiterating once more that the key to successfully stage-managing an interest in and willingness to discuss M&P issues is nurturing a safe atmosphere. Cultivate an environment where people are comfortable exploring ideas, concerns, feelings, and root impressions they formed over the years as to their reasons for being, and you are on your way to some wonderful exchanges. Keep reminding people that there is no scientifically correct, more-virtuous-than-the-rest answer. If it works for you and does not harm others, it's probably terrific.

In the interests of fostering your own skills at shaping this kind of safe climate for explorations of M&P, here are a few tips for you as an M&P facilitator. I believe that, left to your own devices, you would figure all this out soon enough, given a bit of trial and error. Still, maybe I can save you a little time.

Be a guide. M&P insights are everywhere—point out the relevance, fascination, and value of interpreting lessons about discovering M&P. Okay, maybe "everywhere" is a little extreme, but you certainly can perceive possibilities in lots of places, many of which are unexpected and thus even more exciting. Can you recall spotting one today? Listen to the lyrics of songs (e.g., "One Moment in Time," "What's It All about, Alfie?" and so on). Many surely recall the great ads on the meaning of life run for years by Mazda Motors. These promotions linked the company's production process with the habit of asking good questions, such as "What's it all about?" Mazda gave away copies of *The Meaning of Life,* a wonderful book by Time-Life to anyone who came into a showroom for a test drive and brought a card appearing with print ads on M&P. Many books in both the nonfiction (*Wonderful Life*) and fiction (*Cider House Rules*)* categories focus on M&P—and explore the extent to which life is or is not nasty, brutal, meaningless, or short! Don't overlook newspaper cartoon features (e.g., "The Far Side," "Calvin and Hobbes") and, of course, the richest sources of all, the theater (*Our Town*) and motion pictures (*Dead Poets Society, City Slickers,* and *The Meaning of Life,* to note just a few).

Be passionate! Actually, what I have in mind is encouraging people to think about and nourish their passions. The simplest way to begin to discover the M&P people have created for

---

*A bibliography of recommended wellness literature appears at the end of this book.

themselves in life and whether their life is nasty, brutal, meaningless, and short is to inquire about or otherwise explore their passions in life! What matters deeply to you, how you spend your free time, your pride in avocational pursuits, artistic activities, or hobbies—these are reflections of commitments based on M&P.

Doesn't this make sense? What are some of your own passions?

I think it's crucial to find time, in fact, to make time for whatever you feel most deeply about. Surveys on happiness reveal that the main determinants of happiness are satisfaction with family life, work, and leisure to develop talents. If you or those with whom you are promoting M&P can't think of any passions at the moment, take emergency action to rectify this most hazardous situation. Meaning and purpose are often encased in passions that give us the energy to get out of bed in the morning and the serenity or satisfaction to sleep when we get back into our beds at night. Your passions reveal the living record of your history, somewhat as exposed rock strata affords partial glimpses of the history of life itself. A good barometer of how well nourished your passions are is the extent with which you are satisfied with your family life and friendships, with your work or career, and with the amount of leisure time you reserve to develop your talents. If none of these areas generates any passion, well, maybe there's something to this proposition, after all.

Commit to reason. Don't fall for psychic babble, ESP nonsense, and anything of the kind that defies reason and science—and tell others you feel that way. Next time someone asks "What's your sign?" tell her you think anyone who believes in astrology is a bloody idiot with whipped cream for brains! No, I'm just kidding, that's my style, not yours. Don't be offensive—there are enough of us doing that, already! Just don't pretend to go along if you don't believe in superstition and pseudoscience. Politely mention that you're "hung up on" or predisposed to rational thinking processes. Surely you believe that your judgment is more reliable than extrasensory perception, etc. Your rational faculties will be more helpful in your attempt to live in accord with personal responsibility than a reliance on superstition, D&Cs, or uncritical subservience to mythical traditions and primitive rituals. This tip seems especially applicable to those familiar cultural belief norms to which you were exposed when very young. At the time, you had a limited capacity for observation, a skewed sense of reality, and richly undeveloped faculties for rational thinking. Hopefully, you are better off in all these categories today! All this equally applies to those whom you wish to stimulate and guide ever-so-gently toward a greater interest in M&P.

Orson Welles said, "Man is a rational animal who always loses his temper when called upon to act in accordance with the dictates of reason." Prove Orson wrong, at least in your case: Hold your temper—favor the dictates of reason.

Lighten up. Try not to take things too seriously, including yourself—and encourage those with whom you work and play to adopt a similar attitude. This is very important in the event I'm more or less right on two conditions, namely: (1) that life is nasty, brutal, meaningless, and short; or (2) that life is not nasty, brutal, meaningless, and short. Either way, you surely agree with a part of this proposition, that life *is* very short—the ultimate bottom line is *not* health, wealth, power, fame, thinness, or even living a wellness lifestyle. The objective is not to strike a better deal with Mother Nature via healthy habits in order to age as little as possible, as slowly as you can.

What is it then? What is the ultimate bottom line? Who

knows? Only you can decide, so make it up and put as much energy and time into it as you can find! That's what I'm doing, and encouraging my family, friends, students, business clients, and even a few total strangers to consider.

Look, maybe you should consider for a moment that life is a game. If this is so, then the winner might be the one who dies having enjoyed the most DBRU equivalents.* Follow your best instincts in shaping a wellness lifestyle and maybe you will be around long enough to amass a small fortune in DBRU equivalents.

Summarize a life. You can start with your own, settle on a style you like for this exercise and then use it to help others. Start by writing a sentence or two that you might like to see published with your obituary notice. This is not so weird, you know. Think about it—who, after all, is better qualified? Who is most likely to get it right, you or a total stranger in a newsroom who probably never heard of you and has probably been given incomplete and somewhat erroneous fragments of biographical data about you—and can't sort out the trivial from

---

*For readers not familiar with the *Ardell Wellness Report,* an explanation of the acronym "DBRU equivalent" is in order. DBRU stands for "dead bloated rhino underfoot." Really. You had to be there. Here's a short-version explanation:

A DBRU equivalent refers to the best of times. It is a phrase I coined based on a Gary Larson "Far Side" cartoon. The cartoon depicted buzzards alighting on a deceased critter, a rhino, to be precise. One buzzard remarks to the other: "Just think: Here we are, the afternoon sun beating down upon us, a dead bloated rhino underfoot, and good friends flying in from all over. I tell you, Frank, this is the best of times."

DBRU equivalents, therefore, are "best of times" sensations, even for those not disposed to standing atop decomposing rhinos. My irreproducible research indicates we all need a minimal daily allowance of twenty-three DBRU equivalents.

the really good stuff? This is a job for the star of your life drama. That's you! When doing the exercise with others, tell them to take their time. It's worth mulling for a while. Of course, don't wait until it's too late!

Leading players. Who were the three to five most significant people in your life? These are the folks who, for better or otherwise, provided the preliminary answers until you worked them out for yourself or, if you were lucky, helped you shape your earliest questions about the MOL and ways to find M&P.

How did they do it? In what ways did each of the five affect the way you shaped your life? Compose a sentence or two about each of these people in relation to your story.

What if you never existed? For whom did your life make a difference? Name five and note the impact you might have had on each. This question, you might recall, comprises the key dramatic theme of the ever-popular movie starring Jimmy Stewart entitled *It's a Wonderful Life.* Don't rely on having an angel explain how you shaped certain lives—have a go at it on your own, while you're still here.

The best of times. What were your happiest moments? How difficult is it to identify these periods, experiences, and moments in time? Consider how different you are today, and whether the same experiences would provide similar satisfactions at present. In what new ways might you reach such levels, given the changes in your personality, maturity, interests, and all the rest?

Life crises. What were your greatest crises? What did you learn from them? What do these situations reveal about your paths to where you are now, psychologically and otherwise?

On second thought. Would you choose the same job, career, or profession if you could live life over? Why? What does your reaction indicate?

Changes. What other changes would you make in any area of your life if you could play back the tape and start again?

My wonderful traits. What qualities do you have that you most value? Robert H. Lichtenbert, producer of a newsletter on "The Meaning of Life,"* identifies seven qualities of a "meaningful person," namely, reflective, caring, personable, autonomous, possessed of a unique identity, socially engaged, and having a broad vision.[4] What qualities do you most admire?

A life theme. Could anyone affix a motto to summarize your existence? If so, what might it be? In my case, I might choose something like "He did love his DBRU equivalents." Or, "He thought wellness was too important to be pursued grimly." Or, "He knew everyone had to die sometime but hoped an exception could be made in his case." As you can tell, I'm still searching for a motto.

Life is not a zero sum game—the fact that you're a winner does not require others to lose, even in a meaningless world. Spanish poet and philosopher George Santayana wrote, "Why should things be largely absurd, futile, and transitory?"[5] and answered that "they are so, and we are so, and they and we go well together." That's just how it is—make the best of it. You can have a fulfilling life and do so not at the expense of others. Thus, life need not be nasty, brutal, or meaningless, most of the time. It will still be short. Sorry.

NOTES

1. My source for the 3.5-billion-year figure is Michael Novak, "How We Know What We Know," *Natural History* (June 1995): 28.

*For information or a subscription, contact 1823 West Barry Avenue, Chicago, Illinois 60657.

2. Stephen J. Gould, *Wonderful Life* (New York: W. W. Norton & Co., 1989), p. 45.

3. Ibid., p. 44.

4. Robert H. Lichtenbert, "The Meaning of Life," no. 23 (July 1994): 1–3.

5. Santayana also wrote, in "Soliloquies," the following: "There is no cure for birth and death, save to enjoy the interval." Both this quote and that in the main text can be found in *The Sense of Beauty* (1892), Santayana's most influential work.

4

Proposition Four

Life's a Very Funny Proposition after All

"He dreamed he was eating shredded wheat and woke up to find the mattress half gone."

Fred Allen

In my opinion, we've had a national *meaning of life* anthem for over eighty years! It was written by an American icon, George M. Cohan, the composer, playwright, and song-and-dance man known as the Father of the Broadway musical. George M.'s songs are as American as apple pie and the flag about which he wrote (for example, "Yankee Doodle Dandy" and "You're a Grand Old Flag"). The MOL song appears in a play entitled *Little Johnny Jones* which Cohan wrote, produced, and starred in way back in 1911. A song featured in the show is "Life's a Very Funny Proposition after All." I play it for friends and sometimes in workshops on M&P as a wellness issue. Trust me—this is the all-time MOL and M&P tune!

119

As the chapter proposition suggests, I think George M. was right on target and way ahead of today's wellness promoters, including myself, in recognizing that life is indeed a very funny proposition when you think about it, which I think you should, often!

The song is included on the cassette entitled *Nipper's Greatest Hits 1901–1920,* produced in 1991 by BMG Music. To spark your interest, here are the lyrics:

"Life's a Very Funny Proposition after All"

Did you ever sit and ponder,
Sit and wonder, sit and think,
Why we're here and what this life is all about?
It's a problem that has driven many brainy men to drink,
It's the weirdest thing they've tried to figure out.

About a thousand different theories the scientists can show,
But never yet have proved a reason why.
With all we've thought and all we're taught
Why all we seem to know
Is we're born, live a while, then we die,
Life's a very funny proposition after all.

Imagination, jealousy, hypocrisy, love,
Three meals a day, a whole lot to say,
When you haven't got the coin,
You're always in the way.

Everybody's fighting, we wend our way along,
Every fellow claims, the other fellow's in the wrong,
Hurried and worried, until we're buried
There's no curtain call.
Life's a very funny proposition after all.

When things are coming easy and when luck is with a man,
Then life to him is sunshine everywhere.
Then the fates blow rather breezy, they quite upset a plan
Then he'll cry—this life's a burden hard to bear.
Though today may be a day of smiles
Tomorrow's still in doubt,
What brings me joy may bring you care and woe.
We're born to die but don't know why or what it's all about.

The more we try to learn the less we know
Life's a very funny proposition you can bet
And no one's ever solved the problem properly as yet.
Young for a day, then old and grey,
Like the rose that buds and blooms
And fades and falls away.
Losing health in search of wealth
As through this dream we tour,
Everything's a guess and nothing's absolutely sure.

Battles exciting, fates we're fighting
Until the curtain falls,
Life's a very funny proposition after all.

Doesn't this song demonstrate what health promoters want people to understand, namely, the importance of making the most of the short time available and to fully appreciate the role of M&P as a framework for a great lifestyle? George M. Cohan has given us the meaning of life song! In poignant rhythm, this song suggests that we sit and ponder why we're here and what it is—and can be, all about. It affirms that theories are limitless and none is provable, that we're going to die no matter what, so make the most of living and don't take luck, ease, sunshine, youth, or life itself for granted. Why let endless stressors get us down? This is it—love life while it lasts. We're all different—we make our way as best we can and it's wise not to con-fuse health with wealth or other passing trifles. Focus on joy and celebrate the moment, until the curtain falls.

Of course, George M. sang it better than I summarized and interpreted it, so do go out of your way to obtain a copy of the song itself. I'm sure you will enjoy it.

COMMENTS BY WELLNESS PROMOTERS

Carol Garzona suggested that an awareness of our mortality is a is a healthy perspective:

> We should hold "death" always before our eyes. Michael Lan-don said that when we are born, someone should tell us at the start that we are dying, so we will learn to appreciate every moment. The last cookie in the dish is extra delicious only because we know it is the last one. Thinking about death focuses our life. Zen stuff.

One of my favorite commentaries was offered Bob Basso, a very funny man himself who travels the world helping Fortune 500 and other organizations lighten up and thereby boost pro-ductivity.

> When I was a little boy, monsters were popping up all over the place—under my bed, in the shadows, the closets, and even on my toothbrush. I was paralyzed with fear. My life was all about running, hiding, and waiting for an early demise at the hands of a great, big, fire-eating, saw-toothed demon. Until my dad, the fire chief, took me aside and gave me the for-mula to reduce all monsters to insignificance. He said, "You've got a choice. You can frown and be frightened and

the monster will eat you or you can look him square in the eye and laugh out loud and watch him disappear."

As I got older, the monsters took on names like fear of failure, vanity, mortgage payments, and depression. Each time I remembered my dad's advice, and so far I haven't been eaten once.

Sometimes the search for M&P can result in unexpected discoveries of wry amusement, as in the following promotional advertisement I spotted last summer intended to promote a news program in Tampa, Florida. The program was introduced as something you should watch to gain insights on the meaning of life: "Can I afford to have fun? The secret is to discover how to get a bigger bang out of life without going broke. See major attractions on a budget. Enjoy the great outdoors without a great big price tag. Learn how affordable family fun can be." Well, that's one way to look at it.

Another professional "funster" who weighed in on this proposition was Dr. Joel Goodman of Saratoga Springs, New York. Joel is an entertainer much like George M. Cohan himself in the sense of promoting humor and play as paths to creativity, meaning, and purpose.

Do what you love . . . and the funny will follow. I love what I've been doing through the HUMOR Project, Inc. since 1977 . . . and I love making a difference. Methinks the key is to do something in life that is fun . . . but not for fun. Our organizational philosophy and my personal values focus on doing good work and doing good at the same time. I've incorporated quotes from others in helping make sense of humor and sense of life. In graduate school Sid Simon [a master teacher] taught me that "It's important to do what you value and value what you do." Victor Borge appeared at our annual international conference—I've been using his quote on our organization's envelopes: "A smile is the shortest distance between two people." I also interviewed Steve Allen for our *Laughing Matters* magazine: "Nothing is quite as funny as the unintended humor of reality." Garrison Keillor passed along this wisdom: "Humor is not a trick, not jokes. Humor is a presence in the world—like grace—and shines on everybody." And, finally, I resonate with Erma Bombeck's notion: "When humor goes, there goes civilization." It's important to take your job seriously and yourself lightly. There's a difference between being a serious professional and a solemn professional. I think it's important to take our goals and roles in life seriously . . . but not to take ourselves too darn seriously. We can be in search of excellence and in search of laughter at the same time. It's the little things in life that can add up and make a big difference. It's important to operate as an inverse paranoid—someone who thinks the world is out to do you good. Be open to what our children have to teach us. My own most important mentors are my son, Adam, and daughter, Alyssa. Be open to love and laughter . . . love may make the world go round, and laughter keeps us from getting dizzy.

Physician Dale Anderson of Roseville, Minnesota, also has a bit of Cohan in him and sees the humor–meaning–purpose connection, in fact, this respected physician now practices humor medicine and wellness on a full-time basis, for the health of it.

Feeling, sharing, and teaching the chemistry of happiness has given special meaning to my life. Helping myself, patients, and friends understand that we have a "pharmacy in the head," a personal dispensary of chemicals that helps add days to our life and life to our days. By helping others access this chemistry of endorphins (morphine-like chemicals), I facilitate "inner uppers" that make us high on life. Medical science has now measured and shown that how we act affects body chemistry. Our chemistry, in turn, defines how we feel. Thus, the MOL for me in this, my third 30-year period, derives from encouraging everyone to write his or her own prescription for a true head start by laughing for the health of it.

For distance runner Scott Douglas of Boston, life's funny enough if you have a formula for the MOL, which he seems to have: "For the record, the MOL is 100-mile weeks, good friends, and a big bowl of rice and beans every so often."

Veronica Pick of Newark, Delaware unconsciously follows in George M. Cohan's footsteps with this playful perspective on M&P:

Take it easy, have fun and be silly. Play, play, play!!! Be heart smart—believe in yours. Spread your smile around and laugh a lot. Fill your day with passion and play. Listen to the silence from time to time. Fight for your right to leisure! FDR was right: "The only thing we have to fear is fear itself." The secret to happiness is to feel playful everyday. So P.L.A.Y.—Put Leisure Around You!

Who better to continue the tradition of George M. Cohan than stand-up comedian and wellness humorologist Izzy Gesell of Northampton, Massachusetts?

Two ships sailed in a harbor—one going out on a voyage, the other coming into port. People cheered the ship going out, the ship sailing in was hardly noticed. Seeing this, a wise man said: "Do not rejoice for a ship sailing out to sea, for you do not know what terrible dangers it may encounter. Rejoice, rather, for the ship that has reached shore, bringing its passengers safely home." And so it is in the world. When a child is born, all rejoice; when someone dies, all weep. But, it makes as much sense, if not more, to rejoice at the end of a life as at the beginning. For no one can tell what events await a newborn child, but when a mortal dies he has successfully completed a journey. (From the Talmud)

Bud Wallace of Naples, Florida expressed his approval of George M. Cohan's sentiments as follows:

I am floating on a breeze. I have no destiny or at least none delineated as of now. However, I am always ready to pounce when destiny gets close! As you know, destiny changes every five to seven years for us normal people.

I relate to the Cohan proposition because a lot of people I know, myself on too many occasions, take themselves much too seriously and get screwed up in the process. You can understand the meaning of life if you employ the analogy of a baseball batter: You judge what comes your way and strike at what you think will be the best balls to hit. That's the MOL! It, too, changes every five to seven years. Even though they're limited, you do get lots of at bats.

So, make the best of it all and don't swing at the first pitch.

UNTIL THE CURTAIN FALLS

So we don't live forever. Big deal. You always knew that and so does everyone else. Unfortunately, we all tend to put this potential unpleasantry out of (conscious) mind and that leads to occasional periods of apathy, boredom, and the like. How might you go about stimulating others on occasions while managing to remind yourself to stay on track by celebrating this funny proposition, life, as much as possible?

Well, I'm sure you have quite a repertoire already but here are a few tips for your review. They are more about perspectives and processes than specific actions, since your situation will be absolutely unique given your peculiar background and style of doing things.

Ask questions. For starters, consider that you just can't go wrong favoring questions over giving out answers. "Your assignment, if you choose to accept it" (remember "Mission Impossible?"), is to stimulate, not pronounce. The latter is best left to kings, despots, and dictators, none of whom is in favor in this and most western countries as we near the year 2000.

The fact is you're more likely to succeed at prompting others to ponder M&P issues, particularly this funny proposition known as human life, by posing artful questions than giving out your own answers. I think one reason for this rests with the strength of America, namely, our diversity, particularly our multivaried ways of thinking, valuing, and processing information.

Another reason to favor the use of queries to solutions is that, insofar as M&P are concerned, there are no solutions—at least none everyone or even most are going to buy into who have not already chosen their favorite cult! For these reasons, you might consider taking the view that most folks are probably best served when helped to find their own answers. For these reasons, I think you'll find low-key questioning the most promising technique for facilitating self-discovery. If you are still not convinced, ask yourself, "What do I prefer: Invitations to give my opinion or someone else's declarations of how he thinks things are?"

If this notion is true in general, imagine how much more

persuasive it becomes when dealing with fundamental existential issues. This is critical at the workplace and similar institutional settings. Your co-workers will be a lot less defensive in the face of a question than when confronted with a point of view, particularly if different from their own on M&P-related matters. Besides, questions are better suited to group discussion are more likely to lead to new information and can quickly spark additional questions. Eventually, unexpected and useful information, even "answers" for some people, follow.

This might be a good time for you to decide whether your family, school, or company is ready for a meeting on the relationship of healthy lifestyles to MOL questions! Maybe a good way to inaugurate such a discussion would be asking a question! If I were you, I'd consider obtaining a copy of the George M. Cohan song "Life's a Very Funny Proposition after All," playing it at the start of the session and asking: "What's your reaction to this song?" From this you may find the comments soon involve a sharing of notes on ideas about the dimensions and principles of a healthful, purposeful, and fulfilling life, funny though the proposition (life) may be.

Taking chances. At some point, you may find that you are working (or just having fun) with people who have an "anything goes" orientation and are not easily offended. In these instances, you may find it's more challenging to be a bit outrageous, opinionated, risque, and critical than you would ever wish to venture in less intimate, familiar, and safe circumstances. When and if you think these kinds of conditions apply, then you can interject questions that are loaded down with the baggage of your own biases. Recognize that this is the case, that you are offering your own "pointed" questions and that you are not doing so as an infallible representative of God, in fact, you could be blowing smoke!

Here is a specific example from my own experience in facilitating a discussion with friends who know I'm an outspoken secularist, hostile toward D&Cs, and barely able to contain my dismay with those who use fear and guilt and other exploitative tactics to tell people how to think on vital wellness issues of M&P. In short, this is an example of how I "blow smoke" discussing M&P with others similarly demented.

I think you'll see that a question-based presentation on M&P as a wellness issue need not be overly theoretical and lacking in comic overtones.

Okay, everybody, let's discuss your reactions to a few questions I have on this funny proposition we're living called life. How do you react to one or more of these questions, or parts of those questions that contain multiple questions?

- If some religions did not promote a belief in Satan, would there be any forms of devil worship? Would this mean there would be no satanic cults? If so, would the world be poorer without images of or devotions to the Evil One? Or, would the absence of devil worship and satanic cults be a net gain to society? Before you decide, think of the fun we had as children watching movies based on these ideas—would we not be horror-impaired without devils to populate our childhood nightmares?

- Why do we call people who seem to take leave of their senses charismatics? Do these folks seem to display charisma, in your opinion? What might be a better term?

- How would society be different if there were no religions? What if nobody believed in a God—would that mean the end of infidels?

- If there is a God, what must she/he/it think of all the different religions and myths that exist to honor, worship, obey, sacrifice for, and otherwise follow? Which ones would God favor, and why? Would God, in your opinion, send money to Oral Roberts? Join the "700 Club"?

- Do you think there's life beyond the Milky Way and, if so, do you think they're having fun? Do they have religions?

- Does the U.S. Constitution protect your right to ask questions like this? Are these kinds of questions appropriate at all times, some of the time, or never? Should such questions be put to students in public schools? If nonbelievers satirize religious beliefs in the exercise of their free speech, does this mean they are religious bigots?

- Do Americans (or anyone else, for that matter) have a right to speak critically of any religious tenet they wish to challenge, parody, blaspheme, offend, defame, or otherwise address, as critically as they wish? (This is not to suggest that doing so is polite, but rather to focus solely on whether such speech should be protected in a free society.)

I personally believe "blasphemy" is a victimless crime if ever there were one, but that's just my opinion. Still, I didn't get struck by lighting when I wrote it, which seems encouraging. Fortunately, it is not an offense which can be prosecuted in my country with our secular government, unlike in Pakistan and Israel, to note only two of countless theistic-oriented nations where blasphemy is indeed a serious civil offense. At present, at least in the Western portion of our planet (but not in the past—as you might recall from the history of the Inquisition), the authorities won't arrest you for speaking like an infidel. Yet, a word to the wise—be nice! A recent book (*Blasphemy: Verbal Of-*

fense against the Sacred from Moses to Salman Rushdie*) notes that old laws against blasphemy remain on the books in at least five states in America, as well as in the United Kingdom! It's something to think about. Especially if you're planning a trip to London (they still have The Tower, you know).

Naturally, there are other questions that might warrant framing for wellness discussions that have nothing to do with M&P. After all, isn't there more to life than meaning and purpose? Does everything have to *mean* something or serve a purpose? Certainly not. Still, when you listen to George M. Cohan singing about life and what a funny proposition it is, you might find yourself pondering a lot of questions that do.

Cheers.

---

*Leonard W. Levy (New York: Alfred A. Knopf, 1993).

5

Proposition Five

Everyone Has Made Decisions about M&P; Unfortunately, Many Either Are Unaware of Their Choices or Are Uncomfortable or Resistant to Discussing Their Interpretations.

"For all creatures the ultimate purpose of life is passing on one's genes; once that is done, there are few evolutionary reasons for sticking around."

Caleb Finch

I don't know who Caleb Finch is or was, or where I encountered this quotation, but I would like to think you have lots of reasons to "stick around" after passing on your genes, assuming you've passed any along so far. After all, you probably have reasons for living that transcend evolutionary motives. I certainly hope so.

The intent of this proposition is to suggest that M&P motives are formed at an early age, but are usually not consciously developed under anything like a "meaning of life" banner. Would you agree? Does this generalization fit with your experience? Do you feel as I do that deeply held ideas about M&P are too important to be left in the subconscious? Other things being the same, does it not seem desirable to have a high degree of tolerance for and comfort with your beliefs about why you're here—and a capacity to articulate these interpretations? Can you easily discuss your prevailing thoughts about your purposes in life?

I have been asking my students these kinds of questions for over a decade. I also invite friends and colleagues to comment on M&P issues and interact with audiences all over the world on similar matters. The reaction is and has always been rather consistent—some folks love to talk about M&P and are quite capable of doing so. The other 95 percent can't and aren't. Why is this? Is it just a personal thing (i.e., people decide something like "I'm well aware of my M&P choices and am comfortable discussing these ideas, but not with this turkey"), or is this consistent with your experience?

Let's check the reactions to this proposition from a sampling of wellness leaders and practitioners.

COMMENTS BY WELLNESS PROMOTERS

Deb Jones of Vancouver agreed with the proposition and explained why she believed it was true. She suggested that many folks find M&P questions a bit frightening, and prefer not to deal with the matter:

> Making a decision is a conscious process of weighing the options and choosing what works best. I think most keep themselves too busy to dig deep enough to think this through, weigh their options and make decisions about M&P. I know

many people who surround themselves with people constantly and never spend the time alone that it takes to ask these questions. Perhaps it's too scary. Perhaps this is why many people are afraid to be alone.

Of course, this is not true for everybody, as Dennis Elsenrath humorously explained in responding to the proposition:

Am I aware of my choices about M&P? You mean, why am I here? What do I think regarding what it's all about? Doesn't everyone know the answer to these questions? What's the matter with these people? We are here to learn about wellness, that is, how to live a responsible, meaningful life that is fulfilling, helpful to others, and leaves the earth a bit better than it was before we arrived. How can we do this? Well, everyone must decide for himself (unless he's a woman, in which case she decides for herself). There are zillions of possibilities, but I'll mention five of my favorite ideas about what's important regarding our M&Ps. The first is about relationships. Connections with others matter, so nurture relationships and grow with and from them. Second, being mindful is important, which means to think, choose, and pursue your vision. Taking healthy risks would be a third thing that matters, and enjoying what you do is a fourth. Fifth, I favor avoiding unnecessary pain, though pain is a valuable teacher from which we can learn.

Frank A. Roberts said this about unexamined M&P choices:

Over the years, my M&Ps have become clearer. I'm more aware of these ideas than ever before—they seem to have crystallized into two related thrusts—self-actualizations and self-wisdom. I am beset with numbing possibilities with limited time and energy. I can never fully actualize, say, my tennis talent, without sacrificing other interests calling for my attention. So I ceaselessly reflect on my priorities and then, without proof that this choice is the best use of time and talent, I act. I haven't always, preferring the safety of chronic introspection for the insecurity of action. The unexamined life is not worth living was my favorite call to inaction. Then one day, in a flash of insight, I realized that the unlived life wasn't worth examining.

So now I base my life on a ready, set, go program. I ready through introspection, dialogue, meditation—anything that helps me define my direction. Set is the preparation and training period that prepares me for the go, the action.

All this must be constantly informed by the search for wisdom. I define wisdom as the capacity to differentiate likenesses within differences and differences within likenesses. Wisdom is not a thing that I have. It is rather an aspiration that ceaselessly unfolds.

Naturally, some people are quite clear about their purposes and are willing and able to communicate their path to meaning with no hesitation or uncertainty, as is the case with Gina Oliva of Washington, D.C.:

For me, the key idea [is] to leave the world a better place, in some small, big, or medium-sized way, than it was when you arrived. There is, in fact, a quite easy way to approach this seemingly formidable task. Ask yourself, "What is the one thing about my community, or my profession, or my church, my state, my country, etc., that *really* irks me?" We all have complaints, right? Probably, you could even make a long list! So make your list, prioritize your complaints from most to least irksome. Then, decide which ones to act upon. Remember, even if you are not rich, famous, beautiful or President (or his/her spouse), it doesn't mean you can't have an impact.

Gina further suggests you find a cause:

Your life can have one big, long cause, or many short-term causes or something in-between. Truly, though, to have a cause, to do something about the thing(s) that irks you, will allow you to leave the world a better place.

That, dear reader, is one tried and true way of finding M&P. Happy list-making.

Emina McCormick of Burlington, Vermont suggested that an openness to M&P is invaluable for understanding who we are, for becoming whole, and for gaining the most from experience:

The meaning of life comes from developing our own beliefs. To develop our beliefs and thus find meaning, we must draw upon our inherent resources for becoming whole. We must enrich our inner life, and we must also experience our creative and spiritual qualities. Small fears and limited awareness often keep us from connecting life events, from seeing what they are for, from recognizing their purpose, and from instructing us about our future. By believing in ourselves, being open to experiences and reflections, we can recognize our special identity and harmonize it with the larger identity of the universe. Given such opportunity, the MOL will crystallize from its own nature, revealing our meaning in life.

My learned colleague from Perth, Australia, Grant Donovan, was reluctant to discuss the meaning of or purposes in life, as I noted while introducing his lengthy comments in chapter 1. Over the course of several years, I pestered him for a statement. One day, he explained why he would not give me a statement about meaning in life with these words: "There is no meaning! Just get on with it and stop writing boring meaning of life books!" I knew then he had more to offer on the topic! Later, I got the statement on the "life is meaningless/invent your own M&P" that you read in the context of proposition one. This shows that many people, like Grant with his initial "no meaning" position, actually have a great deal to think about where M&P are concerned—and, if approached properly, will tell you all about it. Lisa Kerr, also of Perth, Western Australia, suggests that struggling for awareness of M&P may not be necessary, that insights will turn up anyway: "Some people need to understand life in order to live it, others need to live life in order to understand it. Whichever way, you'll find your own answer."

Celeste L. Budwit of San Antonio offers a mantralike meditative series of suggestions for discovering unconscious decisions made about M&P:

> The MOL is not binary, an either you have it or you don't phenomenon. We have degrees of MOL. Look for greater meaning, rather than the meaning of life. Who are you in the middle of the night when no one's around? Can you perceive greater meaning when your mind is filled with yesterday's arguments, today's frustrations, tomorrow's worries? Allow your mind to slow down, breathe, and be more aware. Accept others where they are. Don't be critical of those who don't seem to care about M&P. There have been times in your life when you didn't care, and there may be many times when you don't care. Everyone is on one's own path. Celebrate your uniqueness, what turns you on. Celebrate your successes, explore every experience, especially your hunches and intuitions.

Carol Garzona, my zen-friend from Seattle quoted in each chapter, took exception to this idea:

Not everyone has made a decision about M&P. Some (most) are still simply asleep. It is said, "The day when this question arises in your mind is the most important day of your life." And, no matter what happens, you can never unask the question. Once we have asked the question, we must find the courage to ask about how to discover the way that will lead to answers to this question.

First you need to hear about Oz. Then you need to know that it's possible for people like you to go there. Then you need to be shown (you can't find it yourself) the way there. Then you need the courage to start on the path. Then you need perseverance to continue on the path (no permanent resting). Then once you see it, you need drive to go all the way. Actually, *all* of this separation is only in our linear thinking—the way is all of this at the same time (very Zen!).

Is that perfectly clear?

Francie Berg has a less riddle-like view:

Take pleasure in life. Stop and enjoy spontaneous moments of fun. Yes, we'd better. I don't think everyone has to be a deep thinker to live well and love well. I'm willing to let others simply enjoy life and cope with their day-to-day lives. Remember the Myers-Briggs personality typing: we're not all alike. Thank goodness everyone isn't stuck on pondering the meaning of life! The work of the world would stop.

Morton C. Orman, Baltimore, Maryland, took an interesting approach which I'll use to conclude this sampling of wellness leader reactions to the proposition:

Inventing meaning and purpose is what all human beings do. The question isn't are we or aren't we going to do it. The only question is how useful, healthy, satisfying, or fulfilling are the ones we've unconsciously created—or were handed down to us by others.

I'm also very interested in why most people resist looking at meaning and purpose in their lives. It's like a taboo. Just like many people resist the notion that Einstein actually invented $E=MC^2$ out of thin air, we just don't want to confront the fact that as human beings we have this awesome ability to just "make things up" and then live our lives accordingly.

The wellness promoters have offered many reasons to account for public resistance to M&P reflections and discussions, as well as more than a few suggestions for stimulating a change toward greater awareness of choices made and still available. Now let me offer a few tips along these lines. My suggestions are mainly for those who work with others, but some of the ideas can easily be adapted or interpreted for personal use.

TIPS FOR ENCOURAGING AWARENESS

To assist others clarify, open up to, ponder and maybe even discuss their ideas or convictions about M&P, consider some of the following strategies. These are approaches I found helpful on occasions. (Then, on the other hand, there have been times when some of these techniques nearly caused a riot—so be careful! Just kidding.)

One more time—don't call it spirituality! I know I may sound like a broken record here but it's an important point. Explain right away that diversity of ideas is a good thing, that the intent of discussing M&P is self-awareness, and that differences should be celebrated rather than opposed. Be sure to accentuate the nonproselytizing nature of the M&P forum, in your own fashion. Note that any belief system is just fine—this session you're facilitating is not about seeking converts to anything.

Relate M&P to the interests of the organization. See if you can make some connections between M&P and morale, communication patterns, team building, coaching, health levels, or other aspects of the worksite environment affecting productivity advances. Might there be a link with a valued corporate objective or two, such as work satisfaction and productivity? Think about the challenges involved in redesigning tasks and functions to enable work to connect with and celebrate talents, needs, and desires of employees and that sort of thing. What if people were encouraged to develop new and artful connections between their sense of M&P and the work they do? You don't need careful, scientifically monitored, double-blind, cross-over trials or absolute proof to brainstorm such connections; simply allow for the possibility of confluence. It may not transform the organization but it might spark an interesting dialogue.

Use entertaining materials. There's no shortage of great stuff out there on M&P that everyone can relate to and get excited about. For instance, examine the two books produced by Time/Life on the meaning of life, described in the Appendix. Invite co-workers to select readings that most interest them from the hundreds of very brief essays and photos in these books. Welcome the varied interpretations that will come from this.

Identify or, better yet, ask those involved in these discussions to locate M&P insights and messages that they have observed or gleaned from popular culture. A great source is recent movies. Before the brainstorming session to discover an MOL message in a recent show gets underway, give them an idea of what you have in mind by playing one! Select a movie scene that illuminates at least one perspective on M&P. Among my favorites are scenes from Monty Python's *The Meaning of Life* (dancing through the universe while singing about how amazing it all is), the trophy case lecture about mortality and "*carpe diem*" (seize the day) with Robin Williams in *Dead Poets Society* and the glorious dialogue between Billy Crystal and Jack Palance about the MOL while bringing in the herd in *City Slickers*. (In case you missed it, the MOL according to "Curly" is "to find one thing" that you love—and after that nothing else means . . . little.)

Establish discussion guidelines. These should feature such standards as tolerance, confidentiality, diversity, awareness of cultural imprinting, and so on. It is impossible to have discussions of M&P in totalitarian societies. Let people know that freedom of speech is part of what we all appreciate in western democracies, and that this particular workplace is located in such a fortunate political environment. By taking this approach, you help everyone appreciate the fact that freedom is a blessing and tolerance is expected, else they might as well be living in a theocracy or police state. Imagine trying to run a wellness-oriented M&P, humor, or communications workshop with audience participation in Islamabad or Tehran, or anywhere in Europe during the Inquisition! Take advantage of modern times and freedoms—encourage all those present to reflect on the advantages of living in a secular state, no matter what religious beliefs they hold—and then make the most of this fortuitous situation.

Explore the classic M&P literature—and the rest, as well! Viktor Frankl's masterpiece entitled *Man's Search for Meaning,* an account of his experiences in a Nazi death camp, might be a good starter book. It will surely dramatize the value and power of a strong M&P foundation in a time of crisis. Though Frankl's is of almost unimaginable horror, the lessons apply to all. Simply summarizing a story like this helps people appreciate the importance of conscious awareness of M&P, the utility of which is not tied to its validity or widespread popularity. If someone believes in a bizarre religion (some secular types like myself consider this phrase redundant), a conventional faith, or something else that strikes you as an unrealistic world, respect that. It may make perfect sense to someone else—and give strength in adversity. It is best not to use forums on M&P for proselytizing about precisely where other people should go to find it.

As in other areas, timing is important. Initiate M&P sessions after, never before, the basics of health promotion (testing and other risk intervention) have been introduced. In addition to a safe start to your wellness program or simply healthy lifestyle messages and the always smart tactic of engaging in a bit of confidence building, you want to save your best stuff for later! You do want to ensure that the groundwork has been set before innovating in this dimension. Think of it this way—no point in provoking an ecclesiastical food fight when the company wellness program is just getting started and needs all the support that can be mustered for it.

Identify your purposes. Recall the hit movie *Forrest Gump* (a film which critic Julie Salamon described as "resolutely sweet . . . about a man moving through life with a generous heart and an unsuspicious mind"[1]) when Gump asks the MOL question, "Do we each have a destiny or are we floating around on a breeze?" Ask people how *they* would respond to this query.

Validate the inevitability of change. Note how ideas as well as everything else goes through adaptations over the years. Identify four or five key life stages (youth, young adulthood, middle years, etc.) and the "way we were" at these times. Then, explore the activities that were most enjoyed in these long-ago seasons, the people and events that gave the highest satisfactions, and so on. Then inquire as to how these experiences would fit with current mindsets, and what these changed perspectives imply about early ideas on M&P.

Personal assets. What are the strengths, accomplishments, qualities, or achievements that people are willing to identify about themselves? Of what achievements or personal qualities are they most proud? How would they like to be remembered? This is an area rich in possibilities in emotional explorations that address underlying messages of M&P. Ask people to make a mental or other note of themes and predominant purposes that emerge from these reflections. Don't be surprised if you hear comments like "I want to be an agent for change," or "I want to work for justice," and so on. At first, most are quite vague, because it takes time to mull such over-arching concepts. Encourage folks to take a few days, weeks, or months to think about the questions you put to them. Here are some open-ended questions that might be helpful:

- Rank five of the following values as most important to you—supply other values that you think should be on the list:

*friendships	*family	*adventures
*learning	*religion	*serenity
*service	*creativity	*a cause to advance
*intimacy	*pleasures	*success

- Note the extent in which the work you do complements your purposes in life, if at all. How could the gap be closed—and is this feasible to expect?

- What knowledge do you need to obtain in the years ahead if you are to feel more complete and whole?

- In what ways do you think you might be contributing to the betterment of life for others?

- Assuming you are not already 76.5 years or more, what would you like to accomplish by the time you reach this standard, the average American lifespan? (If you're older than this, congratulations on living so long. Kick back, you've probably done enough!)

I plant a few more suggestions for evaluations along these lines while discussing the remaining five propositions. Those included in this chapter, however, should be more than enough to enable you to stimulate people to bring into conscious awareness those decisions they have already made about M&P in their life. Once aware, they can assess, regroup, and make choices that may be more appropriate, satisfying, and easy to deal with and even share with others.

What do you think? I think it's time to entertain another proposition.

NOTE

1. Printed in the *Wall Street Journal,* 7 July 1994, p. A10.

6

Proposition Six

Everyone Initially Obtains His/Her Sense of M&P from Others, Usually Parents. First Impressions, However, Get Fine-Tuned over Time.

"Life is not so bad if you have plenty of luck, a good physique, and not too much imagination."

Christopher Isherwood*

Christopher Isherwood was having us on when he wrote the above quote, of course—imagination ranks right up there with luck and physique! But luck comes first, after all, your initial sense of M&P comes from your parents—that's what the expression "choose your parents wisely" means! This "choice" affects not just your physique but the quality of initial ideas you're going to live with about the meaning and purpose of your life.

---

*This quote was discovered on the internet computer network without any indication of the source wherein the statement can be verified or its context explored. If you said this first, please accept my apologies—and Mr. Isherwood's!

Some get a better start than others—life's not fair, but you already knew that. I hope.

This proposition, like all the rest, is just a point of view. It's not a theory, not a law of nature, not even one of my imaginary discoveries based on bogus double-blind trials of a longitudinal, horizontal, and dignified nature! Naturally, my idea here was to get a rise out of my fellow activists in the business and avocation of promoting and pursuing healthy lifestyles. Following are a few comments they made about this proposition.

COMMENTS FROM WELLNESS LEADERS

Francie Berg was brief, suggesting, "For some [their first impression is] enough. They are comfortable within the general thinking boundaries of their parents, friends, and community. That's okay, as long as they let me and others expand and move on in our visions of what can be."

Jeff Bensky said he thought the proposition "quite interesting":

Being a possibility thinker is crucial for the success of your life, while having a sense of and appreciation for humor is a close second. There are no coincidences. However, you must be fully aware and have peripheral vision to understand it through the discovery process of living. So, I would agree with this proposition that life's meaning definitely evolves.

Carol Garzona was her usual zenish self:

Everyone is born with a map of the path inside of him or her. It's in the spiritual genes. People on the outside only awaken this thing in us (with grace). They don't put it there. Again, Oz—everything you need you've had all the time; the enlightened ones are simply helping reveal this truth.

One of the few truly elaborate reactions to this proposition came from wellness guru Bill Hettler of Stevens Point, Wisconsin. Bill wrote a statement expressive of his M&P at various stages of his life. More than the proposition itself, Bill's response makes clear how dramatic our adjustments to initial impressions must be as life evolves. Bill prefaced his statement with this remark: "As I enter the sixth decade of my life on this planet, I reflect back on my changing perceptions of the Meaning of Life. I have tried to accurately recall my thoughts, feelings and actions as I reached each tenth anniversary of my birth."

Billy Hettler, age 10—Life is play, action, learning, and family gatherings. Exploring the world is a high priority. A new Schwinn Phantom bike, with a built-in horn and light, made my birthday perfect. The purpose of life is to have fun, through action-oriented activities. Television is something primarily for adults. No kid I knew would ever think of going into the house to watch TV. Our play was in the outdoor world.

Gerhard William Hettler III, age 20—Life is independence, intellectual curiosity, sports, legal responsibilities and the mate selection process. Driver's licenses and draft cards help to transition this young adult into the world of social responsibility. College makes the exploration of the meaning of life a legitimate, credit-earning activity. More questions than answers are encountered. . . . The meaning of life is debated in endless discussions that go into the wee hours of the morning. Sports provide a massive outlet for all types of excess energy. Altruism and service to others brings a sense of satisfaction. The mate selection process, having been retarded by religious and community norms, has more to do with sexual learning and establishing one's sexual identity than actually finding a mate.

Bill Hettler, M.D., age 30—Life is parenting and career. It is a jungle out there and now you have your own genetic material to protect. Now there are endless questions from your own children, and you still don't really know the meaning of life. Balance is difficult to manage, even for this former gymnast. You begin to realize that social and community influences can have dramatic impact on your progeny. Life can have more meaning if you work to improve the social groups within your sphere of influence. There are always choices that need to be explored.

Bill Hettler, M.D., age 40—Life is short for some. High school classmates and parents have died. The essentials of life are very clear. Clean air to breathe, clean water to drink, healthy foods to eat, the love of a partner, physical activity for self and family, social support groups and intellectual stimulation are brought into some semblance of balance. The investment of time in nurturing offspring is becoming less a chore and more a joy.

Bill Hettler, M.D., age 50—Life is love. Love is close to home. Money is not the answer. Health really is wealth. Balance is getting easier each year. Altruism still brings a sense of well-being. The purpose of life is to improve the planet for self and your descendants. Balance is more than a handstand.

Judd Allen of Burlington, Vermont, took Bill's idea to another level, expressing culture as the parent that gives the initial M&P:

For the hungry majority, only bread has meaning. As Abraham Maslow so rightly pointed out, self-actualization cannot be considered unless day-to-day survival is first assured. Supportive cultural environments offer both the means and hope of basic physical and psychological security. In addition to security, the culture can provide a wealth of meaning systems, i.e., ways to connect to nature and each other. Family, love, art, work, heroes, and communication all arise from culture. The process of working with others to nurture supportive cultural environments is the greatest source of meaning in my life. To live a life of meaning, dance with the culture.

Neil Schmottlach, head of the Fisher Wellness Institute at Ball State University in Muncie, Indiana, indicated that the adjustments as life evolves became the quest itself:

I consider myself to be continually searching for the M&P of life. Perhaps I should say I am continually refining basic principles that define who I am and who I wish to be. This is accomplished by continually exploring life's options, taking calculated risks and maintaining a strong support system—a support system that features strong relationships, honest emotions, and diverse opinions.

Bob Lichtenbert of Chicago believes our evolution toward greater M&P as life goes by is so important that it should be expressly addressed by the educational process. In addressing this proposition, Bob also discussed the connection between a satisfying sense of M&P and basic health and well-being.

Education should encompass M&P issues in order to help students gain greater confidence and the capacity to discuss the M&P choices made to date. The key to a meaningful life is education, yet, no school that I know of concentrates on educating its students for a meaningful existence. Lack of or insufficiencies in meaning become most apparent later in life (i.e., health problems) but the seeds are sown in childhood. Education for meaning in schools could be so important to a child's wellness, since he or she has little influence on the quality of the initial meanings presented in the home. Yet, these communications will shape the child's self-image and self-esteem, two meaning elements that will have a great impact in later life. To appreciate the power of meaning in life on overall wellness, reflect for a moment on the vital matter of career choice. Your sense of meaning in life directly influenced decisions on paths considered and directions chosen or foregone. Did your sense of meaning urge you toward fulfilling your highest aspirations or did financial return, expediency, pleasing another or something else shape those fateful choices? For many, a dichotomy between needs for meaning and other factors eventually leads to physical ailments (e.g., lethargy and heart problems) and mental difficulties (e.g., depression and anxiety). Unfortunately, there are no drugs, physical therapies, or surgical procedures for curing insufficient meaning in a person's life. To heal mental pain, you must become aware of and satisfied with varied sources of meaning in life. Some obvious secular sources of meaning include fulfilling work, physical skills, service to others (e.g., volunteer work), nurturing relationships, involvement in community, devotion to the arts, pursuit of knowledge, and all manner of creative expressions. At the other extreme, you can accept an institutional expression of the meaning and purpose of life by embracing a religion, joining a cult or, on a really creative note, starting your own religion or cult! If none of these options has appeal, well, you can always go stark raving bonkers in a happy-go-lucky kind of way!

As life goes by, each source of meaning you nurture and/or discover must play an increasingly larger role. While there are no guarantees for an ulcer-free, happy, and fulfilling existence, success in filling your life with some kind of varied if not intense form of M&P comes pretty close.

Charles "Pete" LeRoy of Billings, Montana, sees crises and mini-deaths throughout life as opportunities for insights about M&P, and hints at the possible need for a new profession based on this proposition:

Our lives are filled with "mini-births" and "mini-deaths." How we choose to respond to these events has a great impact on how and who we are—and who we become. I'm often asked "What would you do if . . . ?" type questions. I cannot answer with any degree of accuracy because I have not faced such situations. Who knows, for example, what I might do if the stresses of life really got to me? I cannot know this. What is my breaking point? Hopefully, I will not have one. Hopefully, I will continue to have experiences which add to my perceived quality of life. Hopefully, such experiences will not come at the expense of intentionally detracting from another person's welfare. I believe a new professional is needed, one who helps people make healthy transitions from "mini-deaths" to "mini-births." Then again, maybe that professional already exists. He or she is just called a teacher, a counselor, or a friend.

Virginia Aronson of Boca Raton, Florida, describes her "spiritual awakening" as a journey of sorts somewhat like Bill Hettler's description of life phases, beginning with the death of a parent:

When I was seventeen, my forty-nine-year-old mother died of breast cancer. Less than a month later, I became a vegetarian. I read voraciously about health, including diet, exercise, vitamins, Eastern medicine, and so on. There had to be a way to live a long and cancer-free life. Thereafter, my lifestyle differed markedly from the health-unconscious patterns of my mother. She had smoked cigarettes, considered house cleaning as exercise, served meat twice daily, and adored desserts, especially chocolate. These habits satisfied her soul as well as her body. In contrast, I became a distance runner, a career dietitian/nutrition writer and a vocal and visible advocate for the healthy life. This phase of my identity lasted twenty years, during which time I refueled the running highs with my work of writing, public speaking, advocacy, and role modeling. My whole life was wellness-oriented, or so I believed.

A few years ago, circumstances began to change—the rigid walls of my self-definition began to erode. A nagging hamstring injury sidelined me. The publishing industry began to suffer the depressing economic consequences of our times. And my lust for working in the health field dwindled. While I didn't turn to parfaits and Camels for solace, I did began to move in a new direction. My life required more meaning than the psychological reassurance of fitness and longevity. I felt an emptiness that no amount of carrot juice or endorphin rush could fill. So I began to read voraciously again, this time on matters of the spirit.

I guess one might call this my spiritual awakening. I prefer to think of it as an expansion in consciousness. I still take good care of my body, but now pay equal attention to my soul. My writing has begun to focus on nonphysical topics. I write poetry and recently finished a book on the link between creativity and altered states of consciousness. I've married a man who is healthy, but not by any stretch of the imagination a health nut. We do dine on beans and rice and enjoy long walks on the beach. But we do not focus on our aging bodies, nor fight the natural process of growing older. We feed and exercise both body and soul. Though we worship the body as temple, we do not forget the God and Goddess it shelters and enlivens. My mother knew this, and lived it in her own allotted time and way.

Peg Jordan of Pleasanton, California, also reviewed a M&P journey from first impressions based on D&Cs to the present time of continuous adjustments and fine-tuning:

As a child I was taught the MOL was to do the right thing to avoid everlasting torment. A life of meaning was marked by delayed gratification, occasional guilt-ridden pleasures and being nice at all costs. Sort of a "hell now, heaven later" philosophy. This left me feeling unfulfilled and empty. In my young adult years, I discovered the hedonist-materialist approach to life. Here the MOL was pure self-indulgence. Live while you can, grab all you want, it's all gone tomorrow and so are you, fool. This left me feeling selfish and still rather empty. Then I discovered the great masters of Eastern contemplative thought. They said the MOL is everything and nothing, evident yet unknowable, within reach but never attainable. Meditate on these things. This left me feeling confused—and appropriately empty.

Lately, I've trusted quantum physics as a stomping ground to explore such questions. Today, I've got a brand new MOL to live by. All I have to do is break through the conundrum of chaos to see the interconnectedness of all beings. Try it yourself. Muster up that mental horsepower and you'll soon be cruising on the universe's fractal freeways, seeing patterns in everything from the DNA helix to dreadlocks in Harlem, from a butterfly's flapping wings to a twister in Texas, from a growing ozone hole to a cancerous Australian mole. It's not a bad place to be—a prejudice-blowing, boundary-dissolving place where you steer clear of fundamentalism and finally understand why it's crucial to love all your sisters and brothers.

When it comes to taking care of yourself and promoting

a wellness message, this grand web-of-life MOL has fantastic, far-reaching, and never-ending consequences. In fact, before the quantum physicists theorized their way here, indigenous people caught on to the interrelatedness of "all my relations." In some Native American tribes, there is a tradition of evaluating how your actions would affect your children's children seven generations from now. Consider the possibilities!

The aging senator who pushes a tobacco subsidy one day hears that his precious grandchild developed asthma due to passive inhalation of cigarette smoke. He can blame the nearby smoker, but the quantum physics MOL would demand he ask how his own actions contributed to her incessant wheeze. This is where it gets exciting, where "spirituality" or the inner life meets wellness and the two become blissful bedfellows, when you no longer simply strive for whistle-clean arteries or the body fat of your aerobic instructor. Instead, you take good care of yourself because you know the world can't afford anything else, because we all depend on it, because it's a grand life, because we're all on "your" side, because you are an integral part of the sacred whole—unique, shining, luminous, and necessary. Now that puts meaning in my life.

Richard Tucker of Minneapolis remarked that all people are eventually successful at finding their M&P, and he used the occasion to address the mystery of "immortality":

Just live a life of meaning—that *is* MOL. Seems fairly simple, doesn't it? It means to live in harmony with the natural environment. To be at peace with others. To conduct oneself in a manner that will do no harm. To live your life for the moment; not with immortality in mind or leaving tangible evidence of your existence. It will only crumble. Life after death is for the living. We live in the memories of those we leave behind. This is the true immortality. Life comes from life and death is the toll. Read this at my memorial service: "Though dying now, life's flame yet glows, Casting shadows on tales untold. Remembrances though we hope will come, Of those few deeds that did get done."*

Yes, to have a meaningful life, live a life that others will remember you for what you did, not for what you didn't. Go to a few Grateful Dead concerts. Renew yourself at Stevens Point [Wisconsin] each summer. Fall in love with a beautiful woman. Watch geese fly overhead. Release a [bird] back into the wild. Strive to live a wellness lifestyle in all your dimensions. Give of yourself to others. Be at peace. All these give meaning to life. Don't climb the mountain searching for someone to tell you the meaning of life. It is within each of us. All we need to do is live it.

Over the course of a highly atypical career track, physician John Travis has probed, tested, adjusted, refined, and reinvented M&P on a personal level while at the same time shaping an entire movement as a principal architect of the wellness concept:

I find meaning and purpose through developing deep connections with others. This is a means for me of recreating the lost extended-family/tribal social structure that has been destroyed. . . . A cult of individualism has replaced the extended-family/tribal structure. It fosters the illusion of separation and estrangement. We are a people alienated from ourselves, each other, nature, and the "spirit."

Recreating a structure that brings M&P back into everyday life involves, for me, relating to people as partners in cooperative endeavors. The most exciting structure I work with to facilitate this purpose is the circle. Circles operate in ways

---

*These lines were written by Tucker himself.

which contrast strongly with how most of us relate to others. The norm is rows—in classrooms, meeting rooms, churches, etc. In rows, there is an authority figure up front who dispenses information, advice, and so on. People in row structures often fall into passivity and compliance to authority. Circles, on the other hand, invite, create, and hold magic, the magic that occurs when people act as one body—partners cooperating rather than opponents competing.

Circles *facilitate* (i.e., cannot guarantee, but certainly encourage) a safe space, a sacred space, if you will, where one can be truly heard by others without judgment. At the very least, circle participants are more likely to discern their judgments as projections and avoid laying their personal agendas on others. In circles, people are more likely to respect diversity and differences and to allow conflict to emerge. It can then be resolved rather than suppressed or glossed over, common practices which inevitably lead to resentment and distance.

Circles can be used to honor the dark side in participants, allowing projections to be explored, owned, and integrated, thereby healing the wounds created by authoritarian structures. I believe that circles, balanced with alone-time in nature, can help us remember the path of our evolutionary destiny by recreating an experience of the lost continuum from which we have been separated. It is the way our ancestors lived for millions of years.

I'm dedicated to fostering wellness through recreating societal norms where the illusion of separation is suspended and everyone is embraced as a part of the whole. In this matrix, meaning and purpose become clear for everyone.

Also, I find meaning through caring for my children in ways that foster a return to the continuum—this is a larger context of circle work. One of the ways we can break the vicious cycle of separation is by holding our infants in arms rather than isolating them in containers and letting them cry themselves to sleep alone. This caring process also helps in healing the child within me, a child who sometimes feels lost and confused because he, too, was denied his birthright by the times in which he was born. All this can be reclaimed. This is my passion and commitment, this is where I find M&P.

TIPS FOR WELLNESS PROMOTERS

If the above commentators are on track, if it does indeed pay to make adjustments in M&P impressions as time goes by, then efforts on your part to promote the process make quite a difference. Such initiatives could represent a significant contribution to the life quality of your friends and colleagues.

To review once more how the fact of this proposition probably plays a key role in well-being, here's a recap of some critical links between M&P and good or ill health:

- Meaninglessness or insufficient M&P contributes to poor health status, probably because of low motivation and energy levels.

- Mediocrity of purposes could be a foundational element in haphazard lifestyles.

- Upgrading M&P could increase someone's chances of finding excellence attractive.

- People concerned about advancing their potentials in life probably do not behave in ways that diminish their well-being (i.e., they do not engage in high risk behaviors).

- An active interest in M&P fuels a life-long interest in examining what others have offered on the matter.

- M&P discussions are likely to improve the tolerance and interest levels of the wellness profession, as the materials readily available are potentially fascinating, controversial, and meaningful.

Who are the folks most likely to resist examining their initial impressions of M&P? I can't point them out, but likely characteristics can be imagined. The presence of these factors might alert you to expect a bit of resistance to your efforts to foster value discussions. But, what the heck, try anyway. Look for the following attributes:

- high seriousness;

- lack of curiosity for science, fiction, music, philosophy, or much else, except drugs, sex, the NRA, TV evangelism, or rock 'n' roll;

- resistance to taking responsibility when a case, however spurious, can be made for another's derelictions or failures; and

- a closed mind to M&P and unwillingness to discuss the matter.

Now that you know how to recognize folks who will be your toughest cases, let's entertain a few specific strategies for moving ahead, just the same. Present, in your own words, the following ideas and your variations of them to anyone you wish to involve in the excitement of exploring M&P.

Use it or lose it. Try exercising your way to a bit of M&P. Fitness is not a cure-all but it helps your brain work better (due to the release of endorphins) and gets you out of the "learned helplessness" mode. When you go for a run, bike, swim, or whatever, you can't help but put out of mind joy-inhibiting, negative things that can clamor for your attention. Thus, to get people to glimpse little insights and momentary reflections on M&P, don't pass up a chance to promote some group exercise. Tell them it can be fun—and done with vigor and panache! It's not only good for their bodies; the fact is that joy, adventure, and exuberant aliveness are more accessible in a workout than in passive attempts to philosophize, endure, manage, and otherwise grimly hang on.

The excited pursuit of little insights into M&P is more difficult for couch or, the latest version, internet potatoes. Look—the quest for meaning takes energy! With a fit, healthy body, your friends will have more time to deal with M&P and have fewer nonproductive distractions (e.g., pain, dysfunction, and the like) to deal with.

Downplay the Ironman—go for the little things. M&P, like joy, love, ecstacy, DBRU equivalents, and so on, arrive in everyday, nondramatic forms. You may be disappointed if you put all your focus on the relatively rare, sensational, often once- or twice-in-a-lifetime moments. Some of the worthiest "best of times" sensations come from daily activities. Life provides lots of mini-finish lines. Seek out little flourishes, modest wins, and unheralded victories on a regular basis. It's actually not so hard—all you have to do is invent them and celebrate them yourself. Just be sure to guarantee yourself these satisfactions, agree in advance not to be too hard to please; make your many finish lines easy to cross, as often as possible.

Assign M&P a high priority. Your sense of M&P is, like good nutrition, too important to be considered a supplement. Make it the main course in a wellness lifestyle, treated consciously every day. Otherwise, you might neglect to undertake matters of consequence to M&P except when "there's time available." Time is never just "available" for the important things in life. M&P is important enough—so make time available. It truly matters!

Be just a little morbid! Try to consider, now and then, an obvious fact that we, most of the time, would rather not think about. Consider that we don't have forever—or anything like forever. Let these memorable words from Ecclesiastes dramatize the urgency of assigning a high priority for gaining maximum M&P to enrich your moments: "Whatever is in your power to do, do with all your might. For there is no doing, no learning, no wisdom in the grave where you are going." (9:7–10).

Be vigilant about the possibilities. Maintain a constant, playful vigilance for those things that raise your M&P antennae. Consider the alternative to interest in M&P, namely apathy. Psychiatrist Irvin Yalow, in the monumental work *Existential Psychotherapy* (reviewed in the Appendix), devotes two entire chapters to the adverse consequences of meaninglessness while reviewing clinical research, why we need meaning, and psychotherapeutic strategies for promoting it.[1] Resolve to invest the energy required to update M&P from what you picked up by osmosis in the early years!

The key to being vigilant about M&P possibilities is to expand your ideas of what is meaningful. Challenge yourself a bit. Don't stay with jobs, relationships, or so-called interests that are meaningless! What is "meaningful" is, of course, a subjective thing. You may be a real airhead who finds soap operas or celebrity murder trials profoundly insightful and indispensable if life is to have meaning! (On the other hand, I realize I may be an airhead for failing to recognize that soap operas and celebrity murder trials are actually metaphors for the ultimate quest and do not represent mental grazing on a par with spectator sports.) Meaningfulness, we can agree, is in the eye of the beholder. Thus, be vigilant in finding meaning, in your own fashion.

Get meaningful medical check-ups. I think doctors should add M&P check-ups to standard clinical history-taking. If Dr. Yalow and others are right about the devastating effect of meaninglessness on mental health, why ignore the consequences for physical health? M&P issues are as significant as sleeplessness, blood pressure, body composition, target heart rates, and a balanced diet with lots of fiber and eight glasses of water daily. It's time to reassess the medical model and make changes in focus. This could, however, take some patients a little time to get used to. Imagine your doctor commencing a physical exam by asking, "Have you discovered the meaning of life yet?" Have you ever had a doctor do that? I have not had this experience.

Be your own doctor. Ask yourself right now this question: "What have I done lately that I believe in, that I'm proud of?" Take your time on this. Then, next time you do visit a physician, dentist, or veterinarian—tell her about your progress in gaining a renewed sense of M&P, even if she doesn't have the presence of mind, sensitivity, or temerity to ask!

Recognize that M&P is a can of worms for some. Even discussing, let alone finding, a satisfying sense of M&P is more difficult for some than others. Remember that not all citizens are happy campers. There's a lot of pain, dysfunction, and troubled people out there. Do your best to be patient and understanding.

I'll give you a specific example. A person bereft of an operating, serviceable sense of humor is going to have difficulty "self-actualizing," that is, investing energy in pursuing higher levels of being, since the lower level needs of safety and security are probably not being met.[2]

Read about it. Examining the M&P literature can be highly enjoyable. The experience can provide a sense of wonder and amazement from reflecting upon the struggles of mere mortals to come to terms with their amazing experiences. Even if you agree with the phrase attributed to Kafka ("The meaning of life is that it stops") or the sentiments of my Uncle Raymond ("The meaning of life is to keep breathing"), the quest for meaning will, in the final analysis, be utterly unique. The good news is that a search of the literature for M&P insights can be fun and compelling. It's hard to do this and *not* reflect on the wonderment and joy of the struggles, effortless and ghastly alike, that we mere mortals encounter trying to come to terms with what's going on. The pleasures of the quest for meaning are there, but you must look for them. The bad news, depending on what you come up with, is that if you are not sensitive and careful, your conclusions could get you excommunicated from the Republican party.

Just kidding. A little.

NOTES

1. Irving D. Yalom, *Existential Psychotherapy* (New York: Basic Books, 1980), pp. 419–83.
2. See Abraham Maslow, *The Further Reaches of Human Nature* (New York: Viking, 1971).

7

Proposition Seven

The Most Fulfilling Insights on Meaning and Purpose Are Discovered, Not Revealed.

"If God wants me to do something, he should tell me, not you. Revelation only reveals to the revelee—after that, it's hearsay."
Greg Irwin, paraphrasing Thomas Paine

The intent of this proposition is to reinforce the ultimate wellness virtue, personal responsibility, in this case accountability for your M&P in life—and for how you arrived at these conclusions.

This is not the easiest thing to do. Far simpler is to allow a higher power or, more likely, someone who claims to be an interpreter for a higher power, to reveal your purposes, the meaning of your life.

Not surprisingly, this proposition drew a lot of reaction from the wellness leaders and practitioners. Here is a sampling of the commentaries.

COMMENTARIES BY WELLNESS PROMOTERS

Jamie Martindale of Indianapolis wrote that

> Proposition seven sounds like the latest California ballot initiative, but two corollaries came to mind in reading it:
> 1. These discoveries about M&P can be made anytime and anywhere. The greatest truths are fully evident in even the smallest of places. All the secrets of the universe are evident in every blade of grass, every child's laugh. Each moment in time can become a timeless moment.
> 2. Discoveries can be assisted without turning them into revelation sessions. While proselytizing is an obstacle to M&P, I believe we *can* help others adopt a mindset more open to discovery.

John Miller of Adelaide, Australia, invented his sense of M&P in part through a serendipitous misunderstanding of what someone else said about the MOL. Here's John's story:

> In 1992 the Dalai Lama visited Australia and was interviewed by Paul Lyneham on the "7:30 Report" on ABC television. Lyneham said: "Dalai Lama, I've been in journalism for twenty-nine years and I've always wanted to ask someone this question: 'What is the meaning of life?'" The Dalai Lama shot back, without hesitation, "The meaning of your life is happiness and usefulness." At one stage, I thought he said "happiness and youthfulness" but someone said it was usefulness. Then I thought again that "happiness and youthfulness" fits me very well. Youthfulness is important to me—as is being athletic, fit, and healthy. Then I thought again: Maybe the Dalai Lama gave Lyneham his own personalized response; maybe he has the intuition to give everyone who has

the courage to ask the question, "What is the meaning of life?" a personalized answer. Which leaves a final thought: the next time you see the Dalai Lama, . . . ask him what is the meaning of his life, and see what he says.

This reminds me of a meaning of life joke I heard long ago, attributed to "Kehlog Albran." Somehow, I am a little suspicious of the authenticity of this credit line—aren't you? Anyway, the joke, if you want to call it that (it may deserve more), goes like this:

A priest asked, "What is *fate*, Master?" and he was answered:
"It is that which gives a beast of burden its reason for existence. It is that which men in former times had to bear upon their backs. It is that which has caused nations to build byways from city to city upon which carts and coaches pass, and alongside which inns have come to be built to stave off hunger, thirst, and weariness."
"And that is *fate*?" said the priest.
"*Fate*? I thought you said *freight*," responded the Master.
"That's all right," said the priest. "I wanted to know what *freight* was, too."

Flexibility is a good thing, especially in the face of such weighty matters as revelation, particularly if you are looking for answers outside of your own resources and putting stock in the words of supernatural authorities, mystics, or masters.

Thomas R. Collingwood, a national fitness leader from Richardson, Texas, feels so strongly about exercise that he suspects some M&P is revealed through vigorous training:

I am of the old school. I believe in no pain, no gain. It is not necessarily pain in the physical sense, but there is a "price" for accomplishment and growth. I learned fitness as a matter of survival, first in sport, then in the military and law enforcement and then in maintaining a healthy life. Much of my current work is with at-risk youth who have mistakenly defined themselves as passive victims. I have learned there are no guarantees in life. The single best thing we can do to avoid being a victim (however we choose to define it) is to intensely exercise daily.

The purpose of activity is to reach a goal, to do what you set out to do. That is what discipline is all about. The physical domain is one of the few areas in twentieth century life where one can experience a concrete and honest reality check. The daily workout becomes an exercise in self-control and self-discipline. Physical activity provides a daily dose of control over your environment, even if the rest of your life is in complete disarray. The meaning is in the process, the movement . . . it's a discovery, not a revealing process.

The learning of purpose and meaning through exercise is the laboratory for learning the purpose and meaning of life. The learning is in the doing. If you want to have purpose and meaning, then just do it!

Steve Carrell of Austin discovered the power of love as revealing his sense of M&P:

The body ultimately stops working, no matter how many sit-ups we do. We also often find ourselves knee-deep in conflict, no matter how hard we try to win friends and influence people. But spiritual wellness can transcend the pain and pleasure of physical circumstances. In *Man's Search for Meaning,* Viktor Frankl tells how he discovered transcendental spiritual wellness in the middle of a concentration camp. This experience was his revelation providing Frankl with M&P and the capability to survive the camp.

Fortunately, Frankl's revelation via horror is not the only path for finding the poetic peace that passes understanding. We can discover such life-giving peace through a strong sustainable love that encompasses others and ourselves. Even in a concentration camp, Frankl secured the source for such durable love, possibly because the search lies beyond outside circumstances. Circumstances may influence, distract, and even overwhelm the search at times. But, most will keep looking to satisfy the innate need for inner wholeness.

Actually, the Beatles may have said (sung) it best, as in "All you need is love." But, they wandered over and around all sorts of avenues and alleys looking for answers. Personally, I settle on Frankl's views on love, even if you can't put his material to song in the shower.

George Sheehan III of Ocean Grove, New Jersey, eldest son of the great runner-philosopher of the same name, offered these thoughts on revelation and discovery:

I once saw Richard Feynman [an American Nobel Prize-winning physicist] interviewed on PBS. He remarked that he never trusted, or bowed down to, a uniform with epaulets. I think he was saying what dad [the late George A. Sheehan, M.D.] was saying. That we are in this game of life to become the unique individual we were meant to be. We filter our own truth, in the end.

To "filter our own truths" is to discover the critical elements of meaning and purpose that can animate a healthy and fulfilling lifestyle. It rarely happens this way with revelations, which suffer from being overly broad. Revelations are therefore seldom tailored or filtered in accord with individual variations suited to personal interests and needs.

Richard Keelor of Raleigh, North Carolina, urged discovery of M&P through a willingness to confront changes head-on:

> Be willing to risk change. Go beyond the patterns and superficiality of our ego-driven system. Challenge the status quo in your personal and spiritual existence. And search for the oneness of all life forms. *Finding* your uniqueness is the essence of spirituality. It *may* be revealed, but you still must find it. Furthermore, "it" will never be revealed in useable form by gurus, shamans, scripture or anyone or anything else—you're on your own. You are responsible. You must make the discoveries for M&P, in communion, I believe, with your own best sense of the Divine.

Sandra Fedorovich of Mississippi State (a town in Mississippi) discovered M&P in values:

> Maintaining awareness of values in life involves a . . . continual and lifelong process of discovery. This commitment to values clarification illuminates our investments of time, energy, money, and preoccupation. It allows us an opportunity to refine our vision and make adjustments . . . when there are discrepancies between what we value and our actual existence. Values awareness leads to insight, choices, personal renewal, and a life of meaning.

This doesn't sound like the kind of thing that comes prepackaged, prefabricated, and preordained (i.e., revealed), does it?

Milwaukee physician Bill Gaertner remarked that M&P is discovered by being fully present to life as it enfolds before us each day:

We all spend the first two decades of life being told the M&P of life by parents, teachers, and/or friends. Somewhere in the third decade, we discover the hard way [that] while these lessons may apply to [those people], they are not necessarily all just right for us. We also discover that a lot of our earlier beliefs were wrong, at which point we're in position to discover M&P for ourselves.

Mary Drabbs of Austin emphasized the value of learning as part of this discovery:

Learning about "stuff" gives life meaning for me. Once I discovered the importance of finding out about things—myself, other people, our surroundings, how to do things—I found enough to keep me busy for a lifetime, or more. And I'll enjoy a lot of laughs, and some tears, along the way.

Lisa M. Battaglia of Raleigh discovered the phrase "random acts of kindness and senseless acts of beauty":

This message serves to remind me each day of the greater meaning of my life. It is the little life pleasures that really count and enhance a wellness lifestyle—remembering a friend's birthday; feeding the birds; letting the neighbor's dog take you for a walk; sending postcards to friends and loved ones for no real reason; bringing a surprise to a lonely person; . . . or singing silly songs with a friend as you drive down the road. I find that the more I live by the words of this wisdom, the more meaning I am able to give and receive about my greater purpose in all wellness dimensions (body, mind, and spirit).

Gloria Kotecki of Milwaukee discovered M&P in service to others: "I've enjoyed working with and learning from seniors;

from life's difficulties I've obtained insights or discoveries into who I am and how I can contribute. In this way I have grown and gained real M&P in life."

How else to discover M&P? Julie Lusk of Salem, Virginia, urges relaxation:

> By now, you're probably convinced of the importance of discovering a personal, dynamic MOL which adds richness, balance, and depth to your life. But how?
>
> One way is to relax, become quiet and listen inwardly to arouse the answers that are ready and waiting be be uncovered. Practice deep relaxation; learn to breathe slowly, fully, and smoothly; meditate or do special guided imagery exercises that clear the mind and awaken your intuition and inner wisdom. Try yoga, go for a nature walk, do something creative.

Linda Tharp of Boulder, Colorado, had some interesting observations about the futility of revelation, as follows:

> It is tempting to turn to the priest, minister, fortune teller, friend, etc., who offers to reveal who we are and what we must do and where we should go to make our lives rewarding. But, better that we take the time and expend the energy required to discover our own answers to M&P. When I looked for M&P in what seemed all the right places (church, schools, leaders, gurus, and so on), I came away cold, empty, and emotionally malnourished. Fortunately, I discovered, bit by bit, that M&P were for me to be discovered within myself via intuition, experience, and rational reflection.

Francie Berg, whom we have heard in many chapters, said something that seems a fitting last word on the topic from the sampling of health promoters:

We discover for ourselves—yes but, sometimes it is in the words of others. Suddenly, we read or hear those words and say, "Hey, that's it!" or what we read clicks with another thought to form a new and marvelous revelation. We can hope that through this book, others will find their own inspiration and insight.

Indeed we can hope for that!

TIPS FOR PROMOTING M&P DISCOVERIES

It's easier, of course, to accept an alleged revelation than to think for yourself, but not as attractive or satisfying. This is true for you, I'm sure, but what about others with whom you might want to engage in M&P discussions? Are there ways to put questions and excite curiosities without raising the Devil and piquing defenders of the Inquisition?

What about an end run or diversionary tactic of sorts? Instead of raising defenses by voicing doubts about beliefs that many hold to be revered truths, how about a simple exploration of thinking styles? You don't have to jog into the path of heavy canons à la the hopeless futility immortalized in Tennyson's classic poem "Charge of the Light Brigade"; polite inquiries about ways of pondering things in general could be just as effective, and more peaceful—and thus productive.

Take rationality, for starters. Most would assume that modern people are more rational, logical, or systematic at cogitating than *Homo neanderthalensis* or *Homo erectus,* but are they? Is this the case? How different are we from our predecessors in this respect? Let's get personal—how far have *you* evolved from our prehistoric ancestors, dear reader? Do *you* favor scientific explanations for natural phenomena, or do you prefer revelations from Christian fundamentalist broadcasters who insist they are blessed with the truth by divine sources? Early man did not have some of the advantages we enjoyed as children, such as free speech (or much speech at all, for that matter), geology, astronomy, or biology books and films, science "exploratoriums," museum field trips or interactive lesson plans explaining natural phenomenon in understandable terms, not to mention the electronic wonders available to today's toddlers. But, have we really benefitted from these changes? Well, of course most have, but what about you?

Let's ponder for a moment your assessment of human capabilities and potentials. Do you believe men and women are inherently capable of solving human problems, or must they rely on the good intentions of spirits or acts of the gods that are beyond human comprehension? These questions may seem rude, sacrilegious, or possibly insensitive to some. Personally, I think they explore beliefs critical to rationality or the absence thereof—and it is our right to frame such questions in a free and proudly democratic society. What do you think? Am I rude or worse to pose such questions in wellness workshops? Can you imagine yourself doing so in any public forum? If so, what kind of reaction would you anticipate?

So, how comfortable are you with questions like this? Are they politically incorrect, impolite, presumptuous, sacrilegious, sinful, or what? If none of this seems inappropriate, distressing, or discomfiting, then why do you suppose you have not heard much, if any, discussion along these lines at your workplace?

The Wellness Connection

Most health experts would probably agree that a desirable characteristic of good health is an ability to attain—and sustain—a personally satisfying degree of meaning and purpose in life. I also think most would urge respect for and the cultivation of a scientifically oriented capacity for reason as part of human development. Don't you think so? In my view, these kinds of explorations can be helpful, not hazardous, to your health and the well-being of others, especially in promoting interest in discoveries of M&P. Openness to deliberations of M&P without boundaries for religious sensibilities (without being provocatively disrespectful) is a choice you can make. The choice, however, will be much affected by your background, that is, your early spiritual/religious programming. As an intelligent and free adult in this country, unlike in theocracies such as Iran, dealing with such questions on a rational basis will be acceptable, and is even encouraged, at least for the most part. What's more, doing so can help you shape a thinking style conducive to personal effectiveness. This activity, free of dogma, creed, and propaganda, can stimulate a periodic reassessment. You can assess where you stand on fundamental matters related to your purposes and sense of meaning. Such basics about your thinking patterns, too often left below the surface level of consciousness, affect the way you view your existence. It affects what you decide to believe and thus how you will feel about the most important issues of consequence to the quality of your life and lifestyle. And, of course, what is true for you applies to everyone you may choose to work with in this broad context of M&P.

A Few Leading Questions

Are you ready to consciously shape a thinking style or existential mindset to rationally reflect upon the great questions? Sure you are! These queries deal with who you are, why you're here and what meaning to attach to your being and purposes—what an adventure!

Here's a sampling of questions I came up with, for starters. It's supposed to help people look at their capacity to favor personal discovery about M&P over the revelation "technique." Perhaps you can adapt it for your own applications. Do so and you will be an existential facilitator! However, I have to warn you about something: I have not yet completed my usual pseudoscientific double-blind, cross-over trials of a longitudinal, horizontal, and vertical study of a dignified nature! The inventory is not guaranteed! On the other hand, it was not something revealed to me in any burning or other bushes. In fact, it could be said I made it up. You could say that, since it's true. Still, who knows, maybe it's inspired or something. Please, check it out for yourself and decide if I'm on to something.

This little list of leading questions will also help you decide if you're pleased with your brain. Do you approve of its performance regarding rational versus superstitious or magical processes? Check it out—maybe you'll decide changes (repairs) are in order. Probably not, though.

The Ardell M&P Existential Test

Please enter a check mark at the end of each of the following sentences if the statement made seems true to you regarding what you believe in, favor, lean toward, or are committed to:

1. Applying reason and science to understanding the universe and solving human problems.

2. Enjoying life here and now and developing your talents to the fullest.

3. Common moral decencies, including altruism, integrity, honesty, truthfulness, and responsibility.

4. An open and pluralistic society.

5. Democracy as the best guarantee of human rights against authoritarian elites and repressive majorities.

6. Striving to work together for the good of humanity.

7. Cultivating the arts of negotiation and compromise as a means of resolving differences and achieving mutual understanding.

8. Securing justice and fairness in society while eliminating discrimination and intolerance.

9. Supporting the disadvantaged and handicapped so that they will be able to help themselves.

10. Attempting to transcend divisive parochial loyalties based on race, religion, gender, nationality, creed, class, sexual orientation, or ethnicity.

11. The principle of separating church and state.

12. Protecting and enhancing the environment and avoiding inflicting needless suffering on other species.

13. Deploring efforts to denigrate human intelligence, to explain the world in supernatural terms, and to look outside yourself or nature for "salvation."

14. The cultivation of moral excellence.

15. The right to privacy.

16. The right of mature adults to exercise reproductive freedom, have access to comprehensive and informed health care, to express their sexual preferences, to fulfill their aspirations and to die with dignity.

17. The notion that scientific discovery and technology can contribute to the betterment of human life.

18. The idea that ethics, moral principles, or normative standards to live by are best discovered together, tested by

their consequences, and amenable to critical, rational guidance.

19. The moral education of your children, nourished by reason and compassion.

20. That the arts are as important or as engaging as the sciences.

21. That we are all citizens of the universe and that discoveries still to be made about the cosmos are exciting.

22. Skepticism of untested claims to knowledge but openness to novel ideas and departures from normal ways of thinking.

23. A disdain for philosophies or theologies of despair and ideologies of violence.

24. A preference for optimism over pessimism, hope over gloom, learning instead of dogma, joy rather than guilt or sin, tolerance in place of fear, love instead of hatred, compassion over selfishness, and reason over blind faith.

25. A belief in the fullest realization possible of your best and noblest capacities as a human being.

Interpretation. There were twenty-five statements in the inventory. How many checks did you enter signaling consent, or at least a basic sense that this was pretty much how you think? If you registered twenty or more checks, I could make a case that you're a "humanist," for these statements are all closely based on "The Affirmations of Humanism: A Statement of Principles" which appear on the cover of each issue of *Free Inquiry,* a magazine for secular humanists. If you checked off five or less, some would probably call you a Nazi! Ha—sorry, just my eccentric sense of humor taking over. If you checked between six and nineteen, I have no idea what to call you and besides, it doesn't matter, anyway.

What really matters is what *you* call yourself, or how deeply you respect your capacity to discover things for yourself. Especially M&P.

I hope this proposition was of interest and helpful—let's move on to the next one. Cheers.

8

Proposition Eight

Everyone Is Unique; No Two Humans Will Have the Same View on Meaning and Purpose Although Similarities Are Likely to Outweigh Differences.

Mark how fleeting and paltry is the estate of man—yesterday in embryo, tomorrow a mummy or ashes. So for the hairsbreadth of time assigned to thee, live rationally, and part with life cheerfully, as drops the ripe olive, extolling the season that bore it and the tree that matured it.

Marcus Aurelius Antoninus (*Meditations*)

By sharing a culture, we begin and end with pretty much the same ideas as everybody else in that culture—with a few important exceptions, which, for better or worse, make the qualitative differences, create individuality, and affect the kind of lives we shape for ourselves. Let's look at what some of the wellness promoters said they were living for and ponder a bit what keeps some people from living fully.

COMMENTS BY WELLNESS PROMOTERS

Grady Cash of Sacramento agreed with this observation:

> Everyone is unique with a one-of-a-kind M&P. For example, what was the M&P for George Washington's mother? How about Mother Teresa? Is GW's mom any less important on a cosmic scale even though she only touched the life of one child? (Sure, maybe she had eight kids—give me a little poetic license here!) After all, GW's mom instilled the values that made that little cherry tree whacker the father of the leading superpower in the world.
>
> The idea that some religious guru or seer knows your purpose in life rubs me the wrong way. In my poem [which appears in the chapter that details proposition nine] I wrote, "If given it rings false, you must find it yourself." M&P is so deeply personal that being "told" your purpose smacks of spiritual elitism. Besides, the journey is as significant as the purpose itself.

If our similarities outweigh our differences, maybe life's common meaning can be found in discovering our unique gifts through the search for M&P. Sandra Martin of St. Louis seems to think so:

> Meaning is found in the search for and fulfillment of our purpose. Our purpose is to learn and teach and thereby bring our special gifts to this life. Meaning is derived from spirituality. My belief system is part of my spirituality and it connects me to the universe and all that is in it. My purpose is to work for the good of the universe, as I see "good." Specifically, this purpose requires that I grow in loving relationships and help others in the same way. There are common elements, such as

identifying barriers to loving, intimate relationships. Yet, overall, our business seems to be to draw as close as possible to living, intimate connectedness.

Diane Shine of Lake Geneva, Wisconsin, reminds us that while humans may have problems with meaninglessness, other life forms seem quite clear about what they live for—for example, her dog, Bo, "a master of wellness":

Bo has taught me about the important things in my life. He eats a high fiber diet, gives and seeks affection regularly, is a good listener, is drawn like a magnet to children's laughter, doesn't hold grudges, seeks the company of others when bored or lonely, explores the unknown and savors the known, doesn't smoke, loves unconditionally, plays, then rests, offers comfort to those in need, drinks lots of water, runs through puddles instead of going around them, and makes me smile.

James R. Ward, a world-class triathlete from Seminole, Florida, who is nearly eighty years old, commented on our similarities:

Life derives meaning from our fulfillment of its purpose. The purpose of life for every species of life, animal or vegetable, is to survive and reproduce. Because man is a rational animal, human beings differ from all other species. Because of our brains, survival to us means more than just existing, and reproduction means more than just producing children. Our brain tells us that we will get the most out of life if we live fully and pursue excellence in every aspect— physically, mentally, emotionally, and culturally. Our brain also tells us that we can propagate life most effectively by helping and educating others, not just our own children, but everyone else in the family of man, to live and live fully. By passing on the lessons we have learned from life's experiences, we and the recipients are both enriched. Life is difficult, because it is full of problems and challenges. Our human nature leads us to prefer fun and leisure to work and sacrifice, but it also enables us to dream and aspire to lofty goals. If we sort out our priorities, establish our life goals, devise and pursue programs aimed at the achievement of our goals, we will find ourselves solving life's problems instead of postponing or shirking them. If we get into the habit of accepting the responsibilities and challenges of life, develop the philosophical outlook that enables us to cope with the setbacks we encounter and help others along the way, we will achieve a high sense of fulfillment and self-esteem. Without self-respect, there is no satisfaction or happiness; with it, life can be meaningful.

Our relationship with others is an important factor in giving meaning to life. When I offered to take my seven-year old granddaughter to watch a children's triathlon, she said she would rather compete than watch it, and did so. It was a little thing, but her response added meaning to my life. She knew triathlons are tough and challenging, but she had the right stuff and wanted to accept the challenge. That added to the meaning of life for me.

Some people, like Julie Lusk, either can't decide what the MOL is, or have a multitude of explanations which they believe are common to all:

Life is for opening the heart, tuning into one's true self, honoring our individual differences and oneness, seeking balance and being truthful. It's about loving and sharing and trusting and growing and being mindful and living life joyfully and exuberantly.

Lauve Metcalfe of Tucson, Arizona, sees so much meaning in life that even the *spelling* of the phrase gives us insights:

*M*ake a difference. In your life and others.
*E*nthusiasm. Express it in all that you do.
*A*we. Acknowledge the wonder and surprises of life.
*N*ow. Live in the present.
*I*magination. Encourage your creative parts to shine.
*N*ature. Honor environmental beauty and magnificence.
*G*oodness. Look for the good in things and all people.
*O*bserve. Allow yourself to watch and listen.
*F*un. Laugh, play, create, and let the child within out.
*L*ove. Learn to love yourself and others.
*I*nspiration. Motivate to accomplish great things.
*F*amily. Be connected with people you love who love you.
*E*nergy. Take care of yourself and nurture yourself.

Susan K. Marshall of Houston sounds common themes in few words, suggesting that M&P are found in learning, self-acceptance, love, and being consciously alive:

Life on earth may simply be a training school which affords us the opportunities for soul evolvement by teaching us how to deepen our ability to unconditionally love ourselves and others. So, I guess it's about learning the key for mastery of life on Earth . . . Just Be.

Bob Fellows of Minneapolis describes a few expressions of M&P that seem available to all of us, if in quite different ways:

I find wonder in the first snowfall of winter, the infinity of the universe, the birth of a baby, and the chemistry of two people falling in love. The amazing mystery is not that we can predict the future, but that we can be aware of what's going on around us in the present. Not that we can project our thoughts by "ESP," but the fact that we can think. Not in the answer to the meaning of life, but in our ability to ask the question.

Jacque D. Dunegan of Windermere, Florida, finds meaning in a fashion that probably held true for most parents who lived a few million years before our time (*Australopithicus afarensis*):

Every time I look into my children's eyes, I know there is a reason for me to be here. Only through learning, growing, stretching, really listening, risking, and adapting do I realize the full meaning of my life. If I were preoccupied, angry or depressed, I would miss springtime and its many beautiful moments.

TOO MUCH OF A GOOD THING?

Okay, assume for the moment that we do indeed share more than separates us in terms of ideas about M&P. Does this suggest that if, for some reason, a few opinion leaders suddenly become fascinated with M&P, a wave of public interest will follow? Could this have adverse consequences? For example, if the masses went hog wild searching for meaning, would productivity fall off, leading to a weakened economy, massive unemployment, and riots in the streets? Not likely. Still, can there be too much of a good thing? Is it possible to overdose on meaning and purpose? Think about this—but not too long.

Look, you've been reading for hours about M&P—and you're just a little over half-way through this opus. Do you ever wonder, "Is it possible that I'm over the over the edge a bit?" Maybe you're *overly* passionate about the quest for M&P! Look at yourself! Do you tear your hair out in a futile struggle to make sense of your existence? Do you obsess about why you're here, what it's all about, and what is the point of human existence?

Probably not. Still, you might want to have some fun with this idea. Here's an outline of a survey you can use with other people in exploring similarities and differences. Personally, I never met anyone who seemed to overdose on M&P. For that matter, I never even heard of such a person! Still, I suppose it could happen.

On the other hand, I certainly would not want to be responsible in any way for your having gone off the deep end, existentially speaking. Therefore, here's another quiz. By answering these questions truthfully to yourself (always tell the truth, particularly to yourself!), you can tell if you're becoming an M&P junkie. Sound reasonable? Okay. Please check "yes" or "no" to the following questions:

1. Do you spend more than one hour a day listening to George M. Cohan sing "Life's a Very Funny Proposition after All?"
Yes___No___

2. Has your productivity at home or work slipped as a result of your questing for M&P?
Yes___No___

3. Do you find yourself getting into arguments over the wisdom or lack thereof concerning what others say about M&P?
Yes___No___

4. Do you get angry if your search for M&P is interrupted?
Yes___No___

5. Do you know the names of all one hundred wellness leaders and practitioners who are quoted in this book and, if so, do you plan to visit or telephone most of them in the middle of the night with feedback on the quality of their contributions?
Yes___ No___

6. Are you still mourning the fact that the "Calvin and Hobbes" cartoon was retired by Bill Watterson and thus no longer appears in the daily newspaper?
Yes___No___

7. Do friends and family say that you are too involved in the search for the meaning of life in general or M&P in particular?
Yes___No___

8. Do you find yourself thinking or daydreaming about M&P?
Yes___No___

9. Have you canceled social events or missed meals or sleep as a result of your quest for meaning?
Yes___No___

10. Have you read all of the recommended books on M&P—and a great deal more—in the past several weeks?
Yes___ No___

If you answered "yes" to no more than three questions, you're doing fine. Four to six "yes" answers and you're beginning to lose it. Seven to ten "yes" answers and you're in serious trouble, pal. You could be on the verge of forming a cult! This item was "inspired," so to speak, by a similar quiz written by Los Angeles clinical psychologist Robert Butterworth "to determine if there is too much O.J. in your diet."*

M&P SIMILARITIES

I almost called this book *Life is Meaningless, God is Dead, and You're Next—Big Deal! A Wellness Approach to Meaning in Life.* However, my publisher eloquently hinted that this was not a good idea with these words: "No." Okay, one word.

Still, I'm convinced that, if we could, just for an hour, put aside religious and other differences that separate us, we would discover that we share more notions about meaning and purpose than divide us. If my fanciful title were somehow believed to be true and the statement were put to every man and woman on Earth, with emphasis on the idea that "you'll be dead soon and this is all there is," imagine how most would answer the following questions:

- Are you having enough fun and adventure? Yes___ No___

- Are you excited about something daily? Yes___ No___

- Are you as healthy as you could be? Yes___ No___

- Are you making a difference for anyone? Yes___ No___

- Are you as free as you want to be? Yes___ No___

- Have you done enough to make your life feel rewarding and purposeful? Yes___ No___

---

*The quiz was published in the *Orlando (Florida) Sentinel,* 8 February 1995, p. A5.

These are simple questions, subject to varying interpretations to be sure, but wouldn't you agree that most would answer "No" to these questions? You, thoughtful reader, may have a few (perhaps all) "yes" checks, but I don't think you're very typical. In my opinion, I'd bet against the chances that the representative people unacquainted with meaning and purpose reflections would put an affirmative spin on their answers to these life evaluation questions. But, and this is the important part of the process if you want to adapt this in some fashion for your own purposes, anyone who even so much as ponders these life assessment questions will be more likely to "seize the day" in the future, and a bit less likely to take the day for granted. After all, time is fleeting and we mortals, like Marcus Aurelius, do very well indeed to engage in such existential meditations.

COMMON WELLNESS STEPS
FOR UNIQUE SEEKERS OF M&P

If we share fundamental notions about M&P, as I suggest in this chapter, even if we are unaware of this fact and even if we do not behave in accord with it, then might we also have an inherent, potential capacity to seek health and well-being along common paths? Can we identify common paths that are clearly evident, easily accessible and attractively presented? I think so, and am reminded of this possibility when I ponder the eighth proposition for seekers of M&P. In order to connect the insights of the wellness leaders' statements with our interest in healthy lifestyles or wellness, and the realization that we share so much as a species, permit me to outline basic tips or steps that build upon similarities.

One way to organize these suggestions is to call them a

"twelve-step" program. It seems there are twelve-step approaches for whatever ails or vexes people these days, so let's consider my steps as a wellness program for those too healthy for any other twelve-step program! In a way, doing so is consistent with the philosophy of Alcoholics Anonymous (AA) and other programs of a twelve-step nature so popular today. All recognize that everyone is unique. Yet, these change programs are designed to make the most of the conviction that we share more than divides us and the former makes possible successful programs. AA, for instance, has been helpful, despite its flaws (e.g., reliance on "higher power" rhetoric), for half a century, in large part because it helps people meet a set of needs we all share that are more important than the differences between us.

With that said, here is my twelve-step wellness program that, if followed in your own fashion and adapted or replaced in part in accord with your style and preferences, should nicely complement your quest for M&P in context with optimal well-being. I hope I'm not getting carried away, but I think if we could gain widespread consent to and pursuit of these twelve steps, we would have an epidemic of health in America or anywhere else the steps were adopted. We could balance the budget, pay off the national debt, and add many years and much quality to life expectancy. And see these changes in a year, at most. Maybe even six months!

Without further ado, here are my twelve steps to complement proposition eight.

Step 1. Walk briskly or otherwise exercise to the point of elevating your heart rate for at least thirty minutes daily. If you would rather rollerblade, swim, bike, run, or something else, by all means do so. But, most will find walking the simplest, cheapest, and most convenient of all routines.

Step 2. Find a way to get paid for doing whatever it is you enjoy. Take your time about this—the pursuit of avocations on a part-time basis may be necessary for decades before you reach this marvelous objective. Pull it off and you will never work another day in your life! You will also fully appreciate what the great "father of stress" Hans Selye meant when he said, "There's nothing wrong with retirement so long as it doesn't get in the way of your work."

Step 3. Do what you must to experience at least twenty-three DBRU equivalents daily. (You will recall that DBRU's stand for "dead bloated rhinos underfoot.") In other words, consciously go after those daily little experiences or moments that lead you to feel you're enjoying the best of times that life can offer—daily.

Step 4. Develop a perspective that embraces responsibility for whatever goes well or poorly in your day and enables you to get on with making the best of things given conditions that exist, in lieu of tendencies to blame, excuse, whine, whimper, or shift accountability to someone or something else.

Step 5. Do not rely on the health care system for your health. This so-called system is not about health—it's a huge disease and illness-based business irrelevant to excellent health and a disciplined wellness lifestyle. No matter how expensive or how wondrous doctors, drugs, and the medical system can be when used appropriately, what you do or do not do (in concert with human biology, culture, and your environment) will be the critical variable in affecting the quality of your appearance, vitality and overall health.

Step 6. Exploit the wonders of the unprecedented information age to become an expert in medicine and health, proficient in accessing information that you desire when you want it, capable of using it appropriately, consistent with your best interests. Among the richest resources for those with computers are e-mail, the world-wide web, and state-of-the-art software programs on computer disks.

Step 7. Resolve to go out of your way daily to experience humor, lightness, fun, joy—good times by whatever name you prefer. Laughter and assorted pleasures strengthen your immune system, metabolize bad vibes, and act in 1,001 ways to make your everyday life richer and fuller. Unlike frustrations, setbacks, tragedy, and disaster, however, initiative is needed to bring these sensations up beyond the minimal level of occurrences.

Step 8. Develop a deep and abiding sense of tolerance for diversity of all kinds, especially differences in styles, appearances, religions, politics, values, and opinions at variance with your own. This is one of the most effective ways to eliminate negative stressors that come from unnecessary and futile judgments as well as temptations to try to change people to think or be more like you. They're not interested and you'll never be effective enough at it to make it worth the grief. Even if they were interested and you were magically effective, they might end up worse off than they were before you changed them. Live your own life and wish others well.

Step 9. Find as many people to enjoy as possible and, if you're lucky and maybe charming and wonderful, love, as well. Some of them will probably reciprocate, or at least be nice to you.

Step 10. Be of service to others, for *your* sake. In your own fashion, reach out and make a difference in someone else's life by supporting a cause, helping the needy, working with a kid—anything. Just don't get sanctimonious about it and realize that the greatest beneficiary will be you—it will add to your sense of worth, purpose, and the like. Frankl, Maslow, Yalom, and dozens of other psychiatrists, existentialists, and assorted scholars have urged engagement for mental health. Don't look for or even accept any awards for this, since it makes you feel good to do it; conversely, don't be too overwhelmed by the good deeds of others. I can't see why anybody makes a fuss about Mother Teresa! She's doing what makes her feel good! Mother Teresa is into self-indulgence! Mother Teresa is selfish in being selfless. Fine. Who would complain? Nobody. Who should be impressed? Nobody. I'm not.

Step 11. Find lots of heroes to emulate, in some ways. It's not a good idea to adopt a single hero, for everyone has strengths and weaknesses and only the former are worth copying. Think of traits you admire and the people who manage those qualities with dignity, panache, and flair—or whatever appeals to you. When you want to function at what you consider your best in these areas, think of your hero for that aspect of living. How would he or she deal with this? Then do your version, with the role model (hero) in mind. By the way, when I was writing this book, my hero was Calvin of "Calvin and Hobbes" fame. I would sometimes ask myself, "What position would Calvin take on a proposition or a wellness tip or a statement by one of the hundred wellness leaders? (If you do not remember Bill Watterson's cartoon strip or are unfamiliar with Calvin's style, well, consider this: In vouching for his character in a strip that involved a letter to Santa Claus, Hobbes wrote, ". . . the kid tries to be sort of good if he's not tempted otherwise." I found these words inspirational.)

Step 12. You did not think I would overlook this, did you? Step twelve is to embark on a lifelong quest to determine the meanings and purposes of life, and make this decision primarily in accordance with the rich database of your own life experiences, observations, and reflections. Of course, you might want to mull my ten propositions, as well, but the key is to remain open to adjustments regarding life insights, discoveries, purposes, and personal meanings as new possibilities come along over time.

Well, that's my twelve-step wellness program to round out this proposition. The steps are rather simple, but vast numbers of citizens clearly do not follow most or any of the steps at the present time, which is why we have such a huge medical system. Personally, I plan to give these twelve steps a shot myself! But, I'm pretty unique (deliberate oxymoron), so I may make a few adjustments.

9

Proposition Nine

While Finding Meaning and Purpose Is an Individual Quest, Certain Expressions of Meaning and Purpose Are Worthy for All to Consider.

"If there were an afterlife, Isaac Asimov would have written a book about it by now."

Anonymous

Proposition nine simply acknowledges the value of paying attention to history, art, science, and all the wonders of earned experience available to your eyes and heart. In the last analysis, we are surely alone and must be responsible for our choices. We must each find our best paths for where and how we live, what we do, whom we love, and all the rest. But, there's an opulent, lush, and fertile panoply of possibilities out there for life shopping purposes. Check out the options, special deals, ads, enticements, and blue-light specials. You don't have to buy a thing—but by being in the market for and open to expres-

193

sions of M&P that appeal to you, you will find a lot of material. Many, I suspect, will be worthy of your consideration.

COMMENTS FROM WELLNESS LEADERS

This was one of the more popular propositions, attracting almost as much response as the first proposition that life is without meaning and thus you better get to work inventing some. I'll give you a sampling, followed by some hints for using this idea to stimulate thinking about M&P.

Francie Berg, who had comments on nearly all propositions, had a zinger for this one:

> This is one with which your contributors undoubtedly agree. Otherwise, they would not bother to send their views along to you. Each one of us has found an answer to the M&P of life and think that it is worthy of consideration by your readers.
>
> There are three forms for expressing M&P that seem reasonable for everyone to at least consider. The first is that meaning and joy of life are found in people and human relationships. This includes family and friends and others who inspire and entertain you, for whom you are concerned and with whom you spend time, including all who work for the same causes and who otherwise brighten your days. Second, the MOL comes from living in a place that feels right. For me, that home is western Dakota. I feel I belong to and appreciate this big land, with its panoramic sunsets, clean air, sudden rains, and wide-open spaces marked by buttes and "badlands" rimming the horizon. Third, the MOL is found in the sense of purpose that comes from working for what you believe in. I'm committed to the physical and mental wellness of people everywhere. I'm challenged to work against the injustice,

greed, and dishonesty so typical of the diet industry. For me, M&P comes from a clear vision, a mission, and the belief that I can make a difference through my efforts and net-working with like-minded others. When my work and writing are creative and challenging, it's like playing all day. It's not work! It's what I want to do, even in my spare time.

Since people, place, and purpose bring meaning into *my* life, it is my hope for others that they have strong, loving, free-ing relationships, live in a place that feels like home, and find a life's work that is challenging, fun and fulfilling.

Carol Filkins thinks everyone seeking M&P should at least consider a central place for the quality of connectedness:

My life feels more meaningful when I'm there with people, and they're with me, in the moments of life. Some moments seem obviously important—weddings, celebrations, crises, births, deaths, etc. The thing is, you don't always know what is important to someone else—so treat daily moments as spe-cial, by staying in the moment and being connected to the people you are with. I think it's nearly impossible to be well alone; I need to be connected. Connection doesn't just hap-pen. Sometimes I have to work hard at maintaining connec-tions—scheduling time, planning, working through con-flicts—and it's always worth it. Connections add M&P to my life—and I heartily recommend them as worthy for all to consider.

For many health professionals, the great challenge is pro-moting wellness as a quest for finding meaning in the work one does. Mike Peterson of Newark, Delaware, is an example of this new breed of health educator:

We spend the majority of our lives involved in "work," so it is essential that work be meaningful and purposeful. Perhaps the preponderance of occupational stress results from working in meaningless and purposeless jobs. How, then, can we make work meaningful and purposeful? How can we move away from approaches that are appropriate for beasts (e.g., a focus on immediate gratifications like money, comfort, . . . and other physical attributes) to more purposeful elements of human existence at the worksite? Perhaps we need to focus more than we do on approaches that deal with accomplishment, responsibility, recognition, challenge, and interest. We give grudging acknowledgment to connectedness as an important aspect of personal fulfillment, but traditional organizational and management paradigms promote isolationism, hierarchy and the like which work against connectedness. In fact, the computer station where I'm anchored right now contributes little to social interaction.

Who would question the merit of living life to the fullest, thereby avoiding boredom and experiencing gusto to the max? Certainly not Australian A. P. Daley of Deer Park, Victoria: "I have never been bored. I love life. I'm sixty-two years old and there's so much I want to learn and try. I may not always feel great, but I haven't got time to be sick. I aim for wellness."

For Susan Morrow of Charlotte, North Carolina, connecting with others is a worthy goal and foundation for M&P:

I keep coming back to the idea of connection, communion, and community to find wholeness. In this way, I think we manifest the freedom to discover meaning in life. Through connection, we can avoid cultural distractions, such as the culture's various compulsions, namely, eating or working too much, chemical dependencies, being a victim, compulsive over-exercise, intolerance of others, religious rigidity, and other "hardening of the categories." With connection, we can instead find our meaning via authenticity and an openness to intimacy.

Maureen Dingelstad of Broadway, New South Wales, Australia, mentioned five expressions of M&P that merit consideration by all conscious seekers of M&P:

When you take time to think about it, the list is more or less infinite, but here are some which are very important to me.
1. Finding wonder in everyday things, such as early mornings, clouds, inch-worms, and bird songs.
2. The excitement of new ideas—sometimes one's own—and sharing them with like-minded friends.
3. The satisfaction of learning a new skill and getting better at it—and sharing it with others.
4. The nice warm feeling of really communicating with perfect ease with another.
5. Laughter.

Claude E. Berreckman of Cozad, Nebraska, has a number of specific ideas for finding M&P for all to consider:

The key word is humble. To be compassionate and love one another is the great challenge of life and thus it's meaning! To live a life of meaning is to be forgiving and merciful and never lose your temper. Life is full of gross provocations, but anger and hatred are total wastes of energy. Become involved in this democracy and fight for our freedoms. Be a patriotic American [or Australian or whatever] and your life will have great meaning.

Marcia D. Poe of Belton, Missouri, suggests there's no need to get complicated about all this:

Shop until you drop? Get it while you can? Keep up with the Joneses? You can never be too rich or too thin? The one with the most toys when he dies, wins? NOT! The meaning of life? The best M&P? Learn the lesson! The lesson is that we already have everything we need!!! All we have to do is to recognize it! Have fun with it! BE!

Susan Marshall of Houston reacted to this proposition by consenting that "it may appear to be an individual quest, but is it, really? . . . Maybe our 'souls' evolve here on earth by learning certain lessons, such as the illusion of separateness when in fact we are one—and to love ourselves and others unconditionally."

J. Grady Cash waxes poetic with advice for all to consider. (Let me say that I know Grady Cash, he's not just a kidder):

The meaning of life, it's not hard to find. The problem is, most people just look with their mind.

Each day of your life, if only you'll start, the message rings clear, if you look from your heart.

I won't tell you life's meaning, but I will tell you this, if given without searching, the meaning is missed.

You must search for life's meaning, though you can seek it with help. If given, it rings false. You must find it yourself.

Keep searching for meaning, for if you search at your best, you'll find great treasures along the path of your quest.

Search the lives of great people, the beliefs they held true. If you look with your heart, it could happen to you.

And don't dwell on the past. It just shows where you're from. It's not who you were. It's who you'll become.

Need an option, idea, or suggestion different from all the rest? If so, consider the statement from a beautiful young woman named Jennifer Heart:

When I think about what really brings meaning to my life, I think of things such as relationships, personal fulfillment, triumphs, physical exhilaration, and moments to be remembered as truly peak experiences. When I try to think of a way or a word that brings this all together to explain my life's meaning, I think of those who speak of "wellness orgasms." Then there is only one obvious choice for me and that is to take this one step further and proclaim that, to me, the meaning of life is sex! After all, there is nothing with greater relevance and purpose in life than that which symbolizes the origin of life itself. I invite you all to share in my life's meaning. Enjoy as much safe sex as possible and enjoy life as much as possible.

Deb Jones of Vancouver, British Columbia, focused on passion: "I find M&P in my life by seeking out and doing the things that I am passionate about, both in my work and personal life. I find these are almost one and the same when I'm working at something I love doing!"

Walt Schafer of Chico, California, mentioned four similarities that unite us in seeking our own M&P:

Meaning of life for me lies in blending personal wellness and social commitment. Four guidelines help me in doing this. First, to have visions and dreams of social significance or the common good. Second, to work hard, partly with others, to bring those visions and dreams to reality. Third, to balance that hard work with personal wellness—care of body and spirit, play, friendship, and intimacy. Fourth, to enjoy the process.

Physician Susan Zahalsky of New York City believes that meaningful work that is fun can be a path to peace, love, and joy worthy for all to consider:

Freud said life is about "work and love." I agree. I try to make work fun and meaningful. Seeing patients at a relaxed pace, keeping up with new information in my field (which makes work interesting), and a lot of humor help make work rewarding. I don't own a lot of things. Living below one's means is liberating. It enables me to choose work I enjoy, practice in an ethical way, and not waste energy worrying about money. I try not to pay too much attention to trivial nuisances (they're going to be there every day, anyway); complaining about them drains attention from the important stuff. I have routines and rituals with people I love (for example, Friday evening dinner with my family). I'm working hard at letting go of fear and anger. When I manage to push these negative emotions from my heart, I've experienced the deepest peace, love, and joy that seem to me to be the true meaning of life.

TIPS FOR PROMOTING M&P

I have mentioned before that I suspect you will discover that a set of good questions can be quite liberating in helping people open up to M&P explorations. One way to do this is to make it a game of sorts, perhaps with a quiz.

A quiz is a safe way to introduce the idea of pondering

"What's it all about?" issues. A quiz encourages people to reflect on critical impressions, their own as well as others. In realizing that many unexamined assumptions were formed long ago when you were quite different in maturity, ideology, educational experience, and so on, it's not difficult to conclude that some concepts may warrant a fresh look.

One way I get people engaged in this process is to give my own, somewhat contorted version of an historical tale. I like to review the adventures of King Arthur and his Knights of the Round Table. (Some scholars debate whether there ever was such a person; some think he was a Celtic chieftain when Britain was struggling against Germanic invaders, but in this and other areas, it's fine to believe whatever you like. For purposes of my story, the reality of the tale matters not.)

You're familiar with the tale of those intrepid, steadfast folks who gathered with Arthur about a round table in the fifth century and decided to go find the Holy Grail? The key part of this tale for M&P discussions is that the Knights had a clear and unmistakable purpose. Their purpose was to find The Grail! If the Monty Python movie about this endeavor is scientifically accurate and historically true in all respects, and I choose not to suspect otherwise, then we must conclude that Arthur and his friends were winging it a bit. They had not a clue as to what this special grail looked like, why it was missing in the first place, or what they would do with it when and if it were recovered!

We have to suspect that, for King Arthur and the rest, finding The Grail was not the point. Searching for it was the point, for goodness's sake! This search was the purpose that gave their lives meaning! This could be the key to the whole shebang! Maybe the meaning of life is to search for our own holy grail, regardless of whatever form such an item (i.e., our grail) might assume. It's the quest that matters, not finding the grail.

So, take a moment right now to ask yourself: Are you looking for a grail? Probably not, but you surely have a purpose, right? What is that purpose, that special quest? What is the nature of your holy grail?

Perhaps things have not changed that much since the days of Arthur. Although he and his good and worthy men have, unfortunately, passed away due to fighting, accidents, and old age, they got a lot out of the search for their holy grail while they went after it. It makes you kind of wonder, doesn't it—are you getting enough out of *your* search for meaning and purpose?

A CONSCIOUSNESS-RAISING TOOL

Well, let's check it out a bit. The following questions may help you inventory how things are going. But, please, don't think for a second that someone else can test you for meaning! No way. Only you can decide if your life is meaningful enough—it's completely up to you. This "test" is not really a test at all but a "consciousness-raising tool" meant to spark your interest, just a bit, in grail-related matters, holy or otherwise. As Aristotle or somebody probably noted, "there is a deeper, inexpressible essence to the meaning of life that cannot be defined, is more mystical than substantial, is felt more than found and realized in isolated moments rather than in an all-encompassing set of goals and desires." In any event, the following little quiz by whatever name might help. It might help you, and your associates, reassess and move closer to a conscious awareness of that "inexpressible essence" you harbor about the MOL. Then, if so inclined, you can consider a few adjustments. Enjoy.

Kindly place a checkmark indicating true or false after each question. Unlike your fourth-grade teacher, I won't admonish you to "Tell the truth, be honest, and keep your eyes straight ahead—no cheating!" After all, you're the authority on the most accurate response to each of these questions!

1. My daily life is, for the most part, interesting, pleasurable, and meaningful and my commitments and values extend beyond my own immediate concerns.
True___False___

2. If asked, I can describe how I find M&P and I'm not hesitant or shy about doing so.
True___False___

3. I enjoy all or most of the people with whom I associate, even those who are essentially creeps, blowhards, and misfits.
True___False___

4. I would not make drastic changes if I knew I had just months to live. I may not hang around this dump, but I would still be the same kind of person.
True___False___

5. I'm confident that my existence has had a net positive effect on a number of other people. (Recall the famous scene in which this question is posed in the movie starring Jimmy Stewart entitled *It's a Wonderful Life*.)
True___False___

6. (To prepare for this question, consider a scene in the movie *Forrest Gump*—even if you haven't seen it. In the film, the title character reflects on the meaning of life while standing at his young wife's grave. Gump thinks of all that

has happened and wonders, "Do we have a destiny to fulfill or are we just floating around on a breeze?") The statement, then, is this: I can deal with not having a destiny to fulfill and can live my life just floating on a breeze.
True___False___

7. My work/career/profession contributes to a sense of meaning and purpose, or at least I have enough opportunities to indulge these feelings from my avocational pursuits.
True___False___

8. I can't think of any goals or desires that are preventing me from feeling good about my life and sense of direction that I've long wanted to realize but have put off for one reason or other.
True___False___

9. I spend most of my days doing what I think is necessary, appropriate, and reasonable; I don't feel constrained or stuck doing what others define as "shoulds" that contradict or offend my sense of what's right.
True___False___

10. I'm comfortable with questions about M&P. I don't feel a need to defend certainties or sacred truths.
True___False___

Interpretation/Scoring. These questions or, better yet, your own version of them, should be useful in helping you and others you interact with to ponder if you or they are on track concerning M&P, and help you assess comfort levels with the process of musing about life's M&P. The questions are not scientific in the sense of being double-blind, cross-over, trial tested, validated, or otherwise the final word. The quiz, in other words, does not really assess if you are a happy and fulfilled human being or a moronic, hopeless, lowlife twit!

Still, you don't have to be a genius, a nuclear physicist, or a frequent guest on a cerebral talk show like "Oprah" to sense that mostly "true" answers to these questions are encouraging from a M&P standpoint. Likewise, mostly "false" answers might constitute a possible basis for panic on matters existential. Possibly. Only you know, although, if you put all false checks the folks with keys to loony bins might start looking at you funny.

No matter your score, ask yourself what your grail (holy is optional) looks like and where the search for it might take you in the years to come. Or, better yet, where would you like it to take you?

Stay open to grails, holy or otherwise.

10

Proposition Ten

The Search for M&P Should Never End Until You Do

"When I die, I want to go quietly and peacefully in my sleep, like my grandfather did, not full of fear and screaming, like all the passengers in his car."

Poster

It seems to me that people in the Middle Ages were wise to be skeptical of Galileo's claims but very foolish to refuse to look into his telescope. One theme underlying all these propositions and the variety of responses to them by wellness leaders is a curiosity about and a willingness to come to some decisions concerning why we are here, what's it all about. We may be skeptical of answers for all humanity (i.e., the cosmic perspective) but most are quite willing to peer into our own telescopes to search for individual M&P.

Of course, some people have no difficulty inventing or accepting cosmic explanations for our presence on Earth, or else-where for that matter (you never know, do you?). This is usually done either on the basis of faith (religion) or empirical observation (science). In the latter instance, physics teaches that molecules tend to assemble into large compounds to increase the entropy of the universe. Biology reveals that the "selfish" gene drives us to continue our species through reproduction and guides us to create conditions favorable for the prosperity of our progeny.

Whether you lean toward a religious, a scientific, or a blend of the two interpretations about why we (and you) are here—or even if you have concocted your own absolutely original conception, I think an openness to the search for M&P should never end until, in George M. Cohan's memorable phrase in the previously cited "meaning of life" song, "the curtain falls" and your show is over.

If you would forgive me for using a phrase I usually apply to the quest for physical fitness, I'll add that you should engage in the search for meaning until the day you die when, for the first time since your birth, you won't need it anymore. Let's see what the wellness leaders and promoters said about this, and then I'll offer a few more tips for your consideration.

COMMENTS BY WELLNESS LEADERS

Karen Wise, a health and fitness specialist in Roswell, Georgia, observed that while we all have a path of meaning, we must search to find it:

> I agree that the search for M&P should never end until we do, but a mistake many make is to focus the search outside of themselves. M&P must first be found within, then it can move

out toward others. If we are constantly looking to other people, things, and events to fulfill us but are not happy with our own contributions, only frustration will follow.

Murray Banks, an Underhill Center, Vermont-based former schoolteacher who now acts as a full-time wellness promoter specializing in seminars for high school educators, noted that he regularly asks audience members M&P questions such as "What do you most value in your life?" and "Do you live by those values?" He described the typical responses:

> Usually health, family, and spirituality rank at the top, well above money, career, or the environment. However, two patterns often arise during discussions. The first is that we value different things at different times in our lives. Proposition ten holds that the search for M&P never ends. . . . I interpret this to mean not so much that you never find it but rather that you find different M&P at different times in your life. When [my wife] and I married and started our careers in teaching, our work and relationship with each other were most valuable and meaningful to us; however, this changed when our sons were born. We didn't drop one purpose and adopt another, we just revised and expanded our perspectives as we evolved. We continue to do so, as M&P is a life-long search. It's also a series of interesting transitions, often building one on the foundation of another, as with a pyramid.

John G. Langdon of Orlando described the search for M&P as neverending precisely because it is beyond understanding, but we grope along anyway and benefit from doing so:

> In a way, we humans are a bunch of loose and fragile parts! We partially rattle, sometimes stumble and fall and, every

now and then, sail smoothly through life. We leave pieces behind here and there, add new parts now and then and move
along. We're searching, it seems, for parts that fit. By nature,
we are incomplete. We are not secure. We must take risks,
and become comfortable being off balance. We must integrate all the parts of ourselves to find the best of our potentials. This requires a special courage, namely, a willingness to
fail. Sometimes, we have to mentally embrace all our diverse
parts! Doing so can be self-love at its best. As life unfolds, we
get better at knowing which parts serve the higher purposes.
One of my favorite parts is my capacity to enjoy seeing others
discover peak experiences. Other parts of ourselves are found
in those moments created by a combination of courage and
curiosity. These moments reveal our true lovableness to ourselves and a fuller understanding of life. Hard work, loving
freely, and staying connected to the natural world lead to
the further integration of our personalities. Living with integrity in a manner consistent with the growth of others will
see you through—even if you never quite understand the
meaning of life.

For Wendy Repovich of Cheney, Washington, the key to enjoying the search for M&P is affection, expressed in hugs:

What I have found so far in searching for M&P is everyone
needs one or more H.U.G.S.—*H*ealthy *U*nlimited *G*ratifying
*S*queezes every day! If we could start a daily "chain letter" of
H.U.G.S. across the world, we probably wouldn't have wars
and conflict anymore.

Karin K. Roberts of Kansas City noted that her search to
date has revealed simply that "the greatest accomplishment is
to die with no regrets (or maybe only a few)."

Joe Taylor of Collingwood, Ontario, indicated that he would prefer not to be *too* successful in his own neverending quest, in that it might be best not to ever know for certain about the cosmic MOL:

> . . . if you knew the real MOL, life wouldn't be fun anymore. . . . One of the great quests that has given life meaning since the invention of fire—the search for the meaning of life— would disappear. Donald Ardell would have to find another topic for his book. Perhaps it could be nonmeaning: "What is the nonmeaning of life?" This would allow people to resume the argument. Maybe good arguments can't be settled. That's why they're good arguments. For starters, what is the meaning of nonmeaning?

Suzanne Tonti of Orlando added this:

> M&P can be found in the commitments we make to ourselves and to others, in the potential we possess and realize. Meaning comes from our ability to love and embrace ourselves just as we are today, as we continue on our journey to becoming more. We find meaning in what we do and how we do it. Meaning comes as well from a sense of discovering more about who we are, the knowledge of who we might like to be, and the joyous acceptance of the difference. But most of all meaning comes from times and experiences we share with the special people we love—those people who love us back and support the core and essence of who we are in the best and worst of times. Friendship, that is life's special gift. Therein lies all the meaning one could ever hope to find.

David Randle of Sandy, Utah, suggests that there are all kinds of ways to find M&P; the search is very much governed by our personality types. The Myers Briggs Type Indicator (MBTI), a popular tool for assessing personality types derived from Carl Jung's theory on becoming a whole person, suggests that motivation, values, or meaning in life is different for different psychological types. Some types find meaning in a sense of belonging, relatedness, or social connections. Some find meaning in being free, being themselves, and acting congruent with their feelings. Others find M&P in being competent, being the best they can be, and striving for quality in all that they do. Still others find M&P in living their lives in relationships where they act out of integrity, love, and creativity. Perhaps the true meaning in life is to be able to find meaning in all of the above and from those meanings to be able to make a difference. Or, a contribution to healing ourselves and healing the Earth so that future generations will have an opportunity to search for their meanings, as well.

Gerald Gergley of Orlando perceives the quest for M&P from the perspective of a life-long athlete:

> Life can be sweet, magnificent, and joyous. It can't be all or any of these things all the time, but through finding your gifts and using them, you can experience the sweet, magnificent, and joyous more than you ever imagined. Personally, I find M&P in chasing youth, not other youths but my own youthful spirit by swimming, biking, and running and being the best ex-fullback-turned-triathlete I can be, regardless of the years, the distractions, the setbacks, or anything else. Find, use, and refine your gifts to an art form and you will discover love, peace, satisfaction, and blessings in this life that will thrill and delight until the end of your time. Good luck.

J. Grady Cash, the wellness poet whose comments on the ninth proposition you probably recall clearly, hints that not only does the search itself never end but, in one form or another, maybe you don't, either:

> I went to one of those New Age things. Past life regression, they called it. Before you start thinking I'm going weird on you, my interest was mostly clinical! As a counselor, I'd learned long ago that perception is more important than fact. If someone thinks he did something in another life and that helps him in this one—fine. Whatever works is okay by me. One of the beauties of life is that we can each follow our own separate paths to find meaning in life. If there were only one right answer, there would be only one religion. Probably a fat Buddhalike Jesus wearing a yarmulke with an Islamic sword in one hand. "If the mountain won't come to Mohammed," he'd say, "Mohammed will come to the mountain, just as soon as I reincarnate, meditate, and feed the sacred cows."
>
> Anyway, I went into this past life regression thing. It was an interesting group of people. An old hippie, one lady wearing rose-colored glasses, some young kids, and a few normal people (normal being those who looked and dressed like me). Our group leader (she called herself a guide) put on some soft music, told us to relax, clear our minds, and wait for a scene from a past life to appear. When it was over, she asked us what we had seen. One young girl was a southern belle riding in a fancy carriage in the pre-Civil War south. One lady was Joan of Arc. Almost everyone remembered him- or herself as somebody famous or rich. Finally, it was my turn. I was a cat, a big cat—probably a mountain lion. I was lying on a rock, high on a bluff out west somewhere. I could see forever. All the territory as far as I could see was mine. I had marked it myself. Then, a prairie dog came out of its hole. I took off after it, caught it, and ate it. Life is good, I remembered thinking. I paused and waited for a reaction to my

story. The lady with the rose glasses looked at me in horror. Mouths were agape around the room. The kids were dumbfounded. Only the old hippie was unfazed. "Far out, man," he seemed to be saying. "I guess you don't get a lot of animals," I ventured. "Noooo, you're the first," our guide replied and quickly moved on to the next person.

When I tell this story, my friends know I'll often make an outrageous comment just to see the reactions I get. "You were kidding about the mountain lion, right?" one would ask. I smile and answer the question with questions. "What could be better than that? You have no enemies. You can bask on a rock in the warm sun. Snuggle beside your mate when winter comes. Catch a gopher when you're hungry. Raise strong young cubs to follow in your footsteps. Your life has meaning. You're a natural part of the cosmos, a single but important thread that helps hold together the majestic tapestry of the world."

They didn't invite me back for another reincarnation meeting. Just as well—I had learned what I needed to know about reincarnation and it isn't necessarily whether you have outstanding parking tickets from a previous life. It's all a matter of perspective. Some people see themselves as unimportant. They want to believe that they are somebody, if not in this lifetime, then maybe in another. They imagine that they were once famous or rich. When will people learn?

Sure, your fate could be better, but it could also be worse. There is beauty around you and in you right now. All you have to do is stop and experience it. And don't waste too much time daydreaming. Life is not a spectator sport, so live the moment. Live it and enjoy it. You'll never have a second chance. Not in this lifetime, anyway. In summary, the MOL has something to do with gophers, or maybe mountain lions!

Lisa De Sieno of De Pere, Wisconsin, concurred with the proposition in this fashion:

The search for M&P is a dynamic process, never ending, forever changing. One day we wake up to find that what once brought us joy and fulfillment no longer suffices to sustain us. How then, do we keep peace with the ever-changing tide of life? Where is the constancy that provides us with nourishment for our souls? These are questions that we must each answer for ourselves. The answer will come to us from a myriad of different avenues—the arts, religions, sciences, philosophies, life experiences, relationships, . . . literature, education, work, laughter, tears, recreation, meditation, imagination, introspection, . . . and the list goes on ad infinitum. Perhaps we discover meaning and purpose through the mystery and awareness of our existence, which essentially (on a deeper level) connects us all as players in the human experience. The key, I believe, is to keep the current of the entire spectrum of our life process charged by formulating questions that propel us toward the answer we seek.

Elaine Sullivan of Dallas perceives her own search for meaning as an evolving part of her journey:

The MOL for me is embedded in mystery rather than mastery. Mystery abounds in the paradoxes I see and experience: pleasure and pain, health and illness, joy and suffering, growth and stagnation, laughter and tears, light and darkness, birth and death. It is this mystery that propels my search for meaning.

I'll conclude wellness leader comments on this proposition with the words of wit and wisdom of Bob Basso. I think you'll enjoy this:

For fifty years I've had daily conversations with God. We talk about everything—why bad things happen to good people, why good people die young, and why he let the Dodgers leave Brooklyn and break my heart forever. I've asked him a thousand times "What is the MOL" and a thousand times the answer comes back the same—"Ask your mother!" I rarely agree with God on anything, but I knew this was his best suggestion yet. Mothers are the only true wise people on the planet because they are the only ones chosen to work with God (or whatever you wish to call the ultimate force) in creating life. So on July 31, 1987, at one o'clock in the morning on the [porch] of her Waikiki [Hawaii] condo, as my father lay dying in the next room, I asked her. She took a deep breath, looked up at a full moon and said, "Stop wrestling with mysteries. Know what you know. Don't hurt anybody and be good to yourself." She paused, then added, "Eat plenty of fruit."

My universe has been clear ever since.

SUMMING UP—A FEW MORE SUGGESTIONS

Okay, you've considered ten propositions from me and 101 additional ideas on M&P from wellness leaders and practitioners. Yet, you remain unsure how, exactly, to address the matter with others? What to do next?

Perhaps you need more, plus a recap, followed by a combination of integrated advice that's entertaining, informative, motivating, and leads to action. Right? Right!

Based on a thorough reading of books listed in the last section in Part Three, the always interesting reactions from the wellness leaders and, of course, my own amazing (if strange) outlook, here are a few more tips for sparking the M&P search! Even if one tip leads to M&P insights, then this book is worth more than whatever you paid for it! Of course, if two or three suggestions resonate for you, then you have really made a sound investment! You may have won the equivalent of a minor lottery!

On the other hand, the above paragraph might be considered the literary equivalent of a political "spin doctor." Just the same, here are a few final personal suggestions. I hope they help.

It's up to you. Recall the formula at the beginning—The meaning of life (MOL) may just be to find a life of meaning (LOM). Your mission, if you choose to accept it, is to make it up! It can and has been said many times, many ways, it's easier said than done. For instance, Robert Burns, an eighteenth-century Scottish poet, wrote, "The purpose of life is a life of purpose." Even Charles Dickens had M&P in mind, I suspect, when he wrote that unforgettable opening line to his autobiographical novel *David Copperfield*: "Whether I shall prove to be the hero of my own life or whether that role will go to someone else, these pages must show." This was Dickens's way of urging responsibility and conscious control of one's own destiny. The way we live each day is the writing we do in the book of our existence. Be the author of the pages of your own life, then your existence will have the meaning you give it. I'm sure you agree that there's little to be said by playing a supporting role in your own drama. Make up meaningful purposes for yourself. I think that's what Dickens was urging when he wrote that first sentence in *David Copperfield*.

Educate yourself about the possibilities. Read a few books mentioned in the bibliography provided. I recommend you start with those written by Durant, Friend, Miller, Frankl, Kushner, Gould, or Yalom. These are my personal favorites; if they arouse your existential interests as much as they excited mine, you'll be hooked, positively addicted, and otherwise fascinated with M&P issues for the rest of your days (and nights).

Give your God a break. Refrain from supplications, after all, you must assume that God knows what He or She is doing and needs no advice or petitions from mere mortals. At least do not ask for something unworthy of the master of the universe, the "supreme being," and so on. To do so is to insult whatever God you claim to believe in. It assumes an interventionist God, which would necessitate a capricious God. When believers do this, it always seems unbecoming, undignified, and embarrassing! Why would such a potent force give a hoot about your petty problems or, for that matter, my truly significant concerns?

Have you ever wondered, when observing an athlete imploring God to help him (and thus hurt the opposition), if that person's God doesn't have more important things to do?" Don't you doubt that God would get involved in field goals or extra points and not get involved in stopping someone from leveling a federal building in Oklahoma City, or anywhere else? Is there a polite way to encourage the devout to refrain from seeking personal favors?

Introduce M&P issues into everyday life. Perhaps M&P can become an ecumenical form of spirituality. Look for opportunities to raise M&P on a regular basis. One of my favorite settings is the dinner party. During a lull in your next dinner party conversation, ask for everyone's attention and say something like this: "Excuse me, but could we all say a few words about the meaning of life? Let's start with you, Gertrude, and go around the table." Be sure to have your own opinion available in case nobody else has any suggestions.

This can work even better with children. The answers are not so important—what matters is helping children learn to think about such matters.

Don't be wishy-washy. Tolerance is one thing, avoidance is something else. If you think a good friend's idea of M&P is goofy, say so, in a nice way. Suppose your friend, responding to an invitation to discuss M&P, comes up with "The MOL is to worship cows, to learn to communicate with the Neptunian Telescope People, and to painfully exterminate all green people from the face of the Earth!" Are you going to say, "Well, that's nice"? No, you will politely try to encourage this person to keep searching. You won't say it, but you can't help yourself if you think along these lines: "Does mental illness run in the family?" In any event, consider reaching out and encouraging your friend to stay open to other possibilities.

On the other hand, if you're convinced that *you* know the MOL or how everyone else can find extraordinary peace and joy through a formula that you invented, please try to resist proselytizing everybody about it. Enjoy it but don't start a movement to convince everybody else that your formula, your way, is best. True believers give conviction a bad name. Is there anyone who hasn't encountered a "born-again" type that you wish hadn't been born in the first place? Try to remember the passage in the "Desiderata" about speaking your truth quietly and clearly and listening to others for they, too, have their story. Consider that there are quite enough proselytizers loose on the planet already, thank you very much.

Check your assumptions. Identify your own biases and be aware that they will be evident to others. You have read ten of my assumptions or propositions in these pages, but there are many more, including a few I consciously recognize! Here are a few others, just to insure that I'm not holding back on you. I assume that:

- Reflections on M&P lead to useful insights.

- A mind open to M&P possibilities improves chances for optimal health and maximum enjoyment of life.

- M&P is more important than most issues discussed at wellness conferences, such as cholesterol levels and body fat.

- A search for the one universally applicable MOL is hopeless and ridiculous; a single cosmic MOL does not fit if we are "insignificant cosmic accidents." That's what Carl Sagan thinks! (Recall his quote which appeared in chapter 1: "We are the custodians of life's meaning. We would prefer it to be otherwise, of course, but there is no compelling evidence for a cosmic Parent who will care for us and save us from ourselves. It is up to us."[1])

- The objective of searching for meaning and purpose is not happiness—finding meaning, being happy are processes, not states of being.

I saw an interesting item about the Dalai Lama recently. This Nobel Prize winner and exiled spiritual leader of Tibetan Buddhists recently addressed seventy-five thousand people in Chicago in the closing event of the Parliament of World Religions. At the conference, he said the purpose of life *is* to be happy! This is in sharp contrast to Viktor Frankl, who frequently emphasized that happiness cannot be successfully pursued, that it must flow from good works. So, take your pick— the experts don't agree. Go for it (M&P) in your own style—maybe it will follow, if not directly, then as a adjunct to other quests.

SUMMARY

Well, it's time to end this part of my own search for M&P via writing about it. I hope some of this will be helpful and most of it was interesting. My purpose was to make your neverending search a bit more interesting and satisfying. I also wanted to help you assist others to explore the same concerns.

There are many barriers to the search for meaning. The greatest might be lack of freedom to pursue the question itself, that is, what are my purposes or what meanings should I invent? Other barriers could be age, lack of sufficient education, financial or other crises, disabilities, lack of support, and so on. Nevertheless, your simple act of asking someone how he or she might obtain added M&P from life could be a contribution, a gift of major consequence.

There are many paths to M&P for yourself and others, including service, adult education classes, work on a cause, affiliation with a dedicated group, and so on.

Ask someone you know to identify a goal, then ask if that goal is consistent with your friend's sense of M&P. This can sharpen thinking on M&P. Or, encourage someone to inventory a dream from this perspective of M&P. This is a technique Viktor Frankl used with success in promoting his method of therapy which focused on the search for meaning, which he called "logotherapy." You might also try asking friends to write out what they want to do in life, what they feel they need to have, to be, or to share with others. Encourage people who try this to keep their pens moving as long as possible, using abbreviations. Ignore practicalities and limitations. Always be prepared to deal calmly but effectively with zealots for dogmas and creeds. Some folks are more interested in advocacy for revealed and absolute truths than harmony for any process of self-discovery. Hopefully, you won't need flak jackets or federal marshals to promote, seek, and enjoy these kinds of exercises. We have the freedom necessary to pursue M&P in America, but we also need to exercise it and to protect it. Stay alert but don't be paranoid!

I'd like to conclude my book as I ended a video I narrated a decade ago for an Orlando television station. The hour-long show, which won two national awards and is still popular today, is entitled "Life in the Stress Lane." It presents the quest for M&P as the heart and, pardon the expression, "soul" of dealing successfully with stress. It dramatizes attitudes and skills that accompany a wellness mindset and urges the viewer to make life a work of art. Many people ask that the final scene be replayed in order that they can copy the concluding remarks. I think the words capture as well the measure of this book; substitute "seek and discover M&P" for "managing stress" and I think you will see my point. So, I'll leave you now with this summary, a part of which was inspired by the Broadway play *Sunday in the Park with George*.

We are a people on the move. We tend to measure our days by how much we've accomplished—we don't like to waste time. As you have seen, it's easy to get caught up in the fast pace of the stress lane. Take the time to learn how to manage that pace so you can survive and thrive.

There is no ready-made stress formula that suits everyone. Exercise alone is not sufficient for managing stress, nor is deep breathing, nor better nutrition, nor meditation. Experiment with any or all of these techniques. Find out what works best for you, make it yours, make it a part of your life. The extent of your power to manage stress is truly vast. But, having the vision is not the solution. As with everything else worthwhile, it takes practice to gain mastery and minimize the time required for good results. The payoffs are worth the investment. Your life is a work of art, and you are the master. To make an excellent design, you need knowledge, skill, patience and commitment. The art of making art is putting it together, bit by bit, day by day, making it happen little by little.

I'm Don Ardell. Good night.[2]

Well, that's it. The end. Enjoy the process, love the journey. Good luck and be well.

NOTES

1. Cited in David Friend and the editors of *Life* magazine, *The Meaning of Life* (Boston: Little, Brown, 1991), p. 73.

2. Information about the WFTV-Channel 9 video "Life in the Stress Lane" is available from AWR, 9901 Lake Georgia Drive, Orlando, Fla. 32817 or by calling (407) 823–5841.

Part Three

Appendix

Resources

"I've found that age is just a matter of mind over matter. If you don't mind, it don't matter."

Danny Dillon*

The following bibliography is provided for readers, including wellness promoters, who are interested in pursuing more knowledge about M&P. While all the listed books are recommended, as a professor I find it hard to resist writing that several should be considered required reading! Yes, you would be tested on a number of these excellent publications, if I could figure out how to pull off such an outrageous idea!

Seriously, I do want to sell you on six very special books that

---

*See *Middle-Age Rage and Other Male Indignities* by Fred Shoenberg (New York: Fireside Books, 1987). This quote isn't in the book, but many others even funnier are.

to me seem particularly appropriate to the issues that led to my ten propositions. Each of these books was helpful to me in developing a strong interest in M&P in recent years and/or better appreciating the significance of M&P as the key wellness issue. Thus, the following reviews are intended to motivate you to make time to read each book. Publishing information (so you can rush out and get your own copies) is included in the bibliography. One or more of these books could have an accelerating impact on your quest for satisfying M&P as part of an optimally healthy and fulfilling lifestyle. Enjoy.

WILL DURANT

What could H. L. Mencken, Sinclair Lewis, Edwin Arlington Robinson, Will Rogers, Mahatma Gandhi, George Bernard Shaw, and Bertrand Russell have in common, besides being dead? The answer is that each of these great men responded to a letter Will Durant sent to more than a hundred luminaries in July 1931. Accompanied by a remarkable (and rather dark) assessment of the lessons of modern science, the letter basically asked: "What is the MOL?" What a terrific letter it was—and the responses from many notables of the 1930s, as well as Durant's own commentaries, were equally marvelous, resulting in the book entitled *On the Meaning of Life*. Both the letter and the responses will be fascinating to all who seek wellness and insights into M&P in our time.

That's the good news. The bad news is that you may have to sell your first born to obtain a copy. Still, I've got mine so who cares! (Ha, just kidding.) If you want to give it a try, you will find this book listed in the bibliography at the end of the chapter. If you have to look around a while to find it, persevere! Good luck—it's worth your best effort to find a copy. (Try bribing the head of interlibrary loans to devote a few weeks to a relentless search on your behalf.)

Durant's letter was designed to arouse the interest of his "famous contemporaries," a term he used to describe the respondents he enlisted as equivalents to my contemporary wellness leaders and practitioners. Durant, too, reached out for contributors throughout America and abroad.

As noted, Durant asked for a response to the MOL question and invited a reaction to his commentary. I borrowed this idea when I asked for a response—and added the ten propositions. In Durant's case, he provided a statement suggesting that the growth of knowledge resulted in disillusionment, which in turn has "almost broken the spirit." It was an amazing commentary but it was also a great way to provoke a response to his survey. Durant listed insights gained from astronomy ("human affairs constitute but a moment in the trajectory of a star"), geology (civilization as a mere "interlude between ice ages"), biology (life as war, just a rude "struggle for existence" among individuals, nations, species, etc.), history ("progress is an illusion," as all glory "ends in inevitable decay"), and finally, psychology (we are at the mercy of heredity and environment).[1]

Still not content, Durant then added an assortment of additional woes and diminishments, including the perspective of philosophy (all that is certain is defeat, death, and "a sleep from which there is no awakening"). In brief, it could be said that Durant's preface or propositions put optimism to rout. Durant's conclusion was that the discovery of truth was "the greatest mistake in human history."[2]

"Discovered truth" led to the same conclusion as the first proposition, namely, that there is no meaning of life, save what we invent. The truth is "there are no delusions to comfort us, restraints to preserve us." Uncovering "truth" has not made us free or happy; on the contrary, it has taken from us "every reason for existence except the moment's pleasure and tomorrow's trivial hope."[3]

If you got a letter like this, wouldn't you respond? Surprising, many did not, for reasons as diverse as not wishing to incriminate themselves or too busy or at a loss to even hazard a guess. However, Durant writes that he was surprised "by the abundance and candor of the replies."

Durant's philosophy on M&P is only partially reflected by his brief if provocative letter to the celebrities. After presenting and commenting on the responses, he elaborated on his own perspectives, noting that the tone of his letter was meant only to guard against "superficial optimism with which men are wont to turn aside the profounder issues of life." Is this not as true today as when Durant wrote the words a half century ago?

There is yet another reason to seek out this book: Who would not be curious to learn what Mencken, Lewis, Robinson, Rogers, Gandhi, Shaw, Russell, and the others opined regarding the meaning of life or how to find meaning and purpose? When you review what they offered Durant, you will discover why Durant chose them—these people were not called "luminaries" for nothing. Fifty years does not date great literature, especially wonderful prose on the MOL! By 2040, these essays will still be hot!

The following are short excerpts from their offerings, which in turn, should be sufficient for an appreciation of and desire to examine Durant's extraordinary collection.

- When faith begins to weaken, "life narrows down from a spiritual drama to a biological episode . . . and shrinks to a strange interlude between a ridiculous birth and an annihilating death."

- Man is but one species among a billion, a passing experiment of Nature who, as Turgeniev said, "entertains no preferences as between men and fleas."

- The simplest MOL then is joy—the exhilaration of experience itself, of physical well-being; sheer satisfaction of muscle and sense, of palate and ear and eye.

- To give life a meaning one must have a purpose larger than one's self, and more enduring than one's life. . . . The MOL lies in the chance it gives us to produce, or to contribute to, something greater than ourselves.

- What you need is not philosophy, but a wife and a child, and hard work. Voltaire once remarked that he might occasionally have killed himself, had he not had so much work on his hands. I notice again that it is only leisurely people who despair.

- You say or imply in your letter that the truth has been discovered and that we are only the worse off, if possible, for that discovery. This is naturally a cause of some chagrin and humiliation for me, for I had heard nothing about it. (Edwin Robinson)

- Of course I haven't thought of anything yet along the philosophy line, but you can never tell what queer things a man might think of during this depression. . . . Well, good luck to you, there seems to be no way to keep people from writing books. The whole thing is a "racket," so get a few laughs, do the best you can, take nothing serious . . . and don't start seeking knowledge, for the more you seek the nearer the "booby hatch" you get. (Will Rogers)

- How the devil do I know? Has the question itself any meaning? (George Bernard Shaw)

In a sense, Shaw was on to something. The first question you have to deal with when seeking the meaning of life or, more realistically, M&P, is to ask, as Shaw did, whether this is a meaningful question. If your answer is affirmative, then you are ready for the next big-time query, namely, what can be a meaningful-enough response to this question? If and when you can respond to your own satisfaction, well, then you might be ready to send out a letter to your own contemporaries, famous or otherwise, seeking their ideas on the matter. That's what I did! As Will Rogers noted, "there seems to be no way to keep people from writing books." I suppose there still isn't.

WENDALL W. WATTERS

Deadly Doctrine, by Wendall Watters, is another wonderful book for wellness seekers on a neverending quest for genuine meaning in their lives. The focus of this work is the common human response to morality, namely, religion. The author, a psychiatrist, examines the psychological price tag of the American addiction to superstitions and cults, the threats that theistic societies pose for democratic freedoms, and the many ways in which rigid doctrines are incompatible with "the development and maintenance of sound health." It's not the kind of thing you're likely to hear in Sunday school!

Dr. Watters sets out to define the link that exists now as well as historically between certain belief systems and chronic low self-esteem, truly immoral or antihuman behavior, alienation from self, sexual maladjustment, failure to achieve intimacy with others, and a long list of other dysfunctions and perturbations. His approach is to review the nature of doctrine and what is known about its contributions to dependency, guilt, gender stereotyping, sexual problems, intolerance, and psychiatric illnesses. Watters concludes that religious indoctrination is incompatible with the psychological growth required for moral development in human beings.

On a hopeful note, Dr. Watters offers a variety of tips for improving your chances for sustaining a wellness outlook, even in a culture steeped in deadly belief systems. Among the wellness tips are the following:

- Think for yourself, particularly on existential issues, no matter how painful or lonely doing so may seem at times.

- Be skeptical about all things supernatural; favor instead your human capacity for reason.

- Resolve to like yourself despite the admonitions of some cults to promote self-loathing, self-debasement, and the myth of innate evil.

- Allow yourself guilt-free sexual pleasures in a responsible way and protect children from mental and emotional toxic addictions.

- Resist absolutism, the need for clear-cut answers to complex problems, particularly doctrinal dichotomies (e.g., good or evil, God or devil, sin or salvation, etc.).

Deadly Doctrine should be of most interest to the devout. A healthy person who is secure, informed, and tolerant in his or her philosophy is not likely to be upset by Dr. Watters's analysis. In a truly democratic society, *Deadly Doctrine* may or may not be of interest, but neither the book nor the good doctor will be seen as a candidate for the burning at the stake.

Curiously, this book is in itself a test of the author's concerns for each reader. Anyone who finds tolerance difficult or impossible or Watters's worldview so offensive as to be stressed, upset, or traumatized may suffer from religious intolerance, addiction, and brain-washing.

STEPHEN J. GOULD

Stephen J. Gould's book *Wonderful Life* addresses several themes—it can be read as art, science, history, or philosophy. Personally, I found it to be about wellness—and the profound significance of chance on the nature of our ideas about meaning and purpose.

At first, wellness seekers might wonder what lessons on M&P might be learned from Gould's book, which is based upon a cross-section of life deposited 570 million years ago on a prehistoric sea floor. For starters, how about humility, wonder, and a strong suspicion that we are here by chance, not some grand design?

Wonderful Life is a story of a new world revealed. It is about the nature of history. It is about the interpretation of a remarkable slice of the fossil record. Amazingly, the interpretation and theories about life were made long after the primary artifacts were discovered and incorrectly classified. *Wonderful Life* is also about a concept called contingency, which will be discussed shortly. In addition, it is about the way we think based on norms and classifications of varied kinds—and what customs can do to our intellectual spread, our choices and our freedoms. Think of the first proposition in reading this book and you realize it is also about the "overwhelming improbability of human evolution." Finally, it is about what might happen if we could "replay" life's tape and what we can learn about our M&P

from asking questions that probe our evolution. For these reasons and the fact that Gould is such a fine writer, this book is highly recommended to wellness seekers engaged in a personal search for M&P.

Gould's tale begins with a discussion of the Burgess Shale in British Columbia, the most important of all fossil locations. Throughout the world the fossil record consists primarily of preserved hard parts (the majority of fossil mammals are known only by their teeth), but this is different. Why? Soft parts are preserved in the Burgess due to the unusual nature of the sudden, catastrophic event that trapped and entombed the creatures in the shale. What was catastrophic for them, of course, is mighty serendipitous for us 530 million years later. Thus, these fossils are preserved in what Gould terms "exquisite detail, down to the last filament of the trilobite's gill, or the components of a last meal in a worm's gut."[4] The Burgess fossils "are precious windows" allowing us to look right into that crucial event in the Earth's history, the flowering of the Cambrian explosion of life forms. As tall as a man and the length of a city block, this small quarry contains the record of the sea floor at the time of an ancient mudslide. Gould claims that it "houses more anatomical disparity than all the world's seas today."[5] He describes how these fossils were mistakenly shoehorned into modern classification groups and then, nearly fifty years after their uncovering, rediscovered for what they actually were, namely, separate phyla the likes of which had not been known to have existed—ever!

Contingency

To understand contingency, think of the classic movie from which Gould takes the title for this book, namely, *It's a Won-*

derful Life, starring Jimmy Stewart. In the film, Stewart's guardian angel replays life's tape without Stewart in it—and demonstrates the remarkable chain-reaction significance of Stewart's life. Similarly, in the chronology of key episodes in history, just a few tiny alterations would have sent evolution plunging down extravagantly varied but similarly plausible tracks in directions that would not have yielded any species capable of understanding the "pageant of its past," or this book, for that matter! Thus, the essence of history is contingency, as is each and every life, including yours. Roll back the tape of your own family's existence a single generation and the world the second time around, without your family, would be unrecognizable. Each life holds what Gould terms "a million scenarios," each perfectly sensible. Little quirks at the outset, occurring for no particular reason, unleash cascades of consequence that make a particular future seem inevitable in retrospect.

Among the breathtaking themes, tantalizing puzzles, and startling facts revealed in *Wonderful Life* that you may not have thought about before are the following questions and concepts:

- Why did it take multicellular life forms (like us) so long to appear? Why did such forms delay their appearance to the point that they occupy less than ten percent of earthly time? Where are their direct, simpler precursors in the Precambrian fossil record?

- Where's the link between progress and predictability? Gould's response would be "there is none!" The history of multicellular life is not a steady rise (a continuum). The history of life shows but "a record, punctuated by brief, sometimes instantaneous, episodes of mass extinction and subsequent diversification."[6] In a literal sense, Gould suggests we "thank our lucky stars" for our presence on Earth, since consciousness would not have evolved "if a cosmic catastrophe had not claimed the dinosaurs as victims."[7] (They prevailed for well over one hundred million years; it's not unlikely that they would have hung on for another sixty million.)

- Reflections on the "staggeringly improbable" series of events that constitute evolution as we know it—and which allowed for the rise of *Homo sapiens*. Any replay of life's tape since the deposit of the Burgess fauna which incorporated what appeared to be the most insignificant, minuscule change would lead evolution "down a pathway radically different from the road actually taken."[8] A corollary would entail recognition of the "awesome improbability" of human evolution. Alter any single event over a six-hundred-million-year period, however slight, and "evolution cascades into a radically different channel."[9]

- One "intolerable" price humans pay for each major scientific gain in knowledge and power is "a progressive dethronement from the center of things" (first noted by Freud) and a sense of "increasing marginality in an uncaring universe."[10] (Perhaps this line of thinking might remind you of the first proposition offered in chapter 1.)

- One of geology's most unsettling facts: the earth has endured for hundreds of millions of years (4.6 billion is the generally accepted number, although our universe is thought to be more than three times older) while human existence is limited to the last geological millimicrosecond, or the last second of the geological year. We are "just one bauble on the Christmas tree of evolution."[11]

- Why we might do better seeking meaning and purpose and the source of our morality "with joy in the challenge" than continuing "to seek cosmic comfort in nature by reading life's history in a distorted light."[12]

- We must care for the environment we have or the quality of our lifestyles will not save us. In one of my favorite Gould expressions (and there are many), he writes the following lines which should be made into a banner and hung on the wall during every wellness seminar: "Groups may prevail or die for reasons that bear no relationship to the Darwinian basis of success in normal times. Even if fishes hone their adaptations to peaks of aquatic perfection, they will all die if the ponds dry up."[13]

Wellness can never work as a hedonistic pursuit of personal indulgence apart from the main. The individual who hones his adaptations to peaks of (nonaquatic) perfection will also die if his ponds (communities) dry up from lack of involvement and outreach. Our sense of M&P must be derived, in part, from our connections with others.

Gould's conclusions are fascinating for all who seek further understanding of the wonders of life and the value of making the most of the wondrous, if unlikely, fact of our existence. All this sets up the kind of observation that makes Gould a guru or at least a giant for those wellness seekers who want to ponder the meaning of their lives on a regular basis: "We are the off-spring of history, and must establish our own paths in this most diverse and interesting of conceivable universes—one indifferent to our suffering, and therefore offering us maximum freedom to thrive, or to fail, in our own chosen way."[14]

Of all the books on the list, this is one of the most interesting and educational. I highly recommend it.

JAMES GLEICK

Genius: The Life and Science of Richard Feynman. If you ever wondered what a talent like Mozart could produce in your own career field (assuming you are not a composer), you might have a similar thought reading about the life of Nobel Prize winner Richard Feynman. *Genius* might at first give you the impression that Feynman's character and talents were otherworldly, but in fact he did have certain qualities seekers of M&P as part of a wellness lifestyle can appreciate. The author notes three qualities that I would put in this category: "A faith in nature's simple truths, a skepticism about official wisdom, and an impatience with mediocrity."[15] In his final moments, Feynman also offered an interesting commentary on the meaning of life, as he saw it:

> . . . I can live with uncertainty and not knowing. I think it's much more interesting to live not knowing than to have answers which might be wrong. I have approximate answers and possible beliefs and different degrees of certainty about different things, but I'm not absolutely sure of anything and there are many things I don't know anything about, such as whether it means anything to ask why we're here. . . . I don't have to know an answer. I don't feel frightened by not knowing things, by being lost in a mysterious universe without any purpose, which is the way it really is as far as I can tell. It doesn't frighten me.[16]

DAVID FRIEND AND THE EDITORS OF *LIFE*

The Meaning of Life: Reflections in Words and Pictures on Why We're Here was produced by David Friend and the editors of *Life.* It is a coffee table book of words and pictures, and most of both are worth examining. Friend and the *Life* staff put the question about life's meaning to no fewer than 750 people. Most of those queried were either famous or distinguished and, presumably, not the easiest folks to contact and persuade to produce a statement or photograph. They included poets, statesmen, artists, philosophers, and street sages. Of the total received, 173 short essays were selected, accompanied by 127 black and white photos. Friend wanted "to capture the essence of human existence"; this may have been a bit ambitious, but it is clear that *The Meaning of Life* at least hints at the range of human experience.

One highlight of the work for me was the author's introduction. In a two-page commentary, Friend explains how the project came about, describes the basis for some of the initial resistance to it, sketches the history of a few predecessor books on the meaning of life (particularly those by Will Durant and Hugh S. Moorhead), reflects on a few statements on meaning, and provides a parting reflection sparked by the passing of several distinguished contributors, particularly Nobel physicist Luis Alvarez, as follows: "His words and his death serve as humbling reminders of the brief span during which we can ponder this eternal question."[17] Other highlights included statements by Carl Sagan, Stephen J. Gould, Jackie Mason, writer and animal rights supporter Cleveland Amory, activist Molly Yard, a gravedigger named Nicholas Vislocky, and, of course, the photographs.

A few years ago, Mazda Motor Company of America gave a copy of this book or its successor version, *More Reflections on the Meaning of Life,* to everyone who filled out a card and visited a Mazda showroom for a test drive. It was a remarkable, provocative, and well organized ad campaign. I did not buy a Mazda despite several test rides, but I did come away impressed that the company asked itself and invited us all to consider some rather profound questions. If, as Friend pointed out in his introduction, yogis ponder the question on lofty cliffs, theologians study and rephrase it, and comedians have a field day with it, why shouldn't we think about it when selecting an automobile and at other times as well, during our brief spans on the planet?

Since you obviously think about M&P more than most, I suggest you have a look at the original and the spectacular follow-up version of *The Meaning of Life* (in color). One obvious benefit of examining so many varied, eloquent, and provocative summaries on the MOL and, more important, what to make of it is you improve your own thinking on the matter; another comes from the sheer pleasure of being immersed in good writing and beautiful photographs.

IRVIN D. YALOM

Existential Psychotherapy, by Irvin D. Yalom, offers an unusual blend of science and literary art. The science will appeal to the professional psychotherapist interested in clinical understanding of and treatment approaches for the ultimate crises of death, freedom, existential isolation, and meaninglessness; the artful ways Yalom addresses concerns rooted in human existence will appeal to everyone else.

Yalom believes that a majority of patients are "bedeviled by a lack of meaning in their lives"; an existential approach to the underlying problem of meaninglessness can, he argues, be as valuable, coherent, rational, and systematic as any other. One reason for the neglect of existential approaches is the difficulty of measuring subjective outcomes, thus, the truly important factors (zest for life, ability to love and care for others, humor, courage, purposefulness, generosity, and engagement in life) are avoided. He offers an existential antidote grounded in meaning and purpose, a solution that should appeal to readers of this book whether their first concern is science (therapy) or art (finding added meaning for a healthier, more satisfying approach to life).

In addition to the major sections on the "ultimate crises" (death, freedom, existential isolation, and meaninglessness), highlights of *Existential Psychotherapy* include:

- A critical appreciation of the impact of those who pioneered in helping us appreciate the role of meaning in life for well-being, particularly Viktor Frankl but also in analyses of the contributions of Camus, Sartre, Schopenhauer and Maslow.

- A review and assessment of tools available to therapists using existential psychotherapy, such as the purpose in life and the life regard indexes.

- Chapters on responsibility and will. Both sections could easily be placed in a book on the wellness concept, for no issues are more central to the challenge of pursuing wellness than these. Yalom's approaches to both are eloquent, comprehensive and insightful. Whereas the entire 524 pages of this epic publication are worth the time it will take for wellness practitioners to examine, these two chapters should be required reading.

Like Frankl, Yalom seems to believe that engagement is the best antidote to or cure for meaninglessness. As to the meaning of life, Yalom suggests that the question is "not edifying," that we do better to immerse ourselves "in the river of life and let the question drift away."[18]

TIMOTHY MILLER

In my experience, many of the best insights for shaping and sustaining wellness lifestyles come from sources outside the medical field and the realm of health promotion, even beyond the banner of wellness itself. One reason for this is that health-related conferences, books, articles, and the rest still seem bogged with medicine, risk reduction, and physical health. Wellness is different from and much more than healing, fixing things, or even preventing problems. It's more than diet, exercise, and stress management. It's an existential concern. It invites questions about the future, such as "How can I get what I want?" This is a way of asking, "How do I discover the meaning of life?" or, more practically, "In what ways might I find deeper meaning and purpose in my work, satisfaction at home, and generally live well?

Well, let's face it, you're not going to get this kind of stuff from an aerobics book! Where, then?

The good stuff in this case can be found in a book by Timothy Miller entitled *How to Want What You Have*. According to Miller, the present is precious but undervalued. Unless you are very exceptional, you long for a future when you think you will be happier because you will have *more*. Unfortunately, *more* will never be enough—you'll still want more. Wanting more is part of your evolutionary heritage, instinctive and inborn. It is the fundamental cause of needless suffering. This unfortunate trait is insatiable and relentless—and it's reinforced constantly by advertising and popular culture. It is manifested by a never-ending quest for more wealth, status, and love.

A little history. How did you get this way? What can you do in order to back off a bit, learn to want what you have and thereby find a bit of peace and a lot more joy, well-being, and other positive benefits, like a successful wellness lifestyle? For starters, you can choose to think, feel, and act in ways that cause the desire for more to gradually become less insidious, relentless, and insatiable. You can, for example, realize that you're not entitled to more. You can also give up the idea that not getting more is a catastrophe or that you have failed if you don't get more. Work on these and other insights that Miller provides and you will improve your chances to truly understand that getting more is not so essential, after all. Then you will not feel tempted to harm yourself or others to succeed at what is inherently futile.

Sound good? It's terrific.

The benefits. Your best chance to experience a better life and be a healthier and happier person is not through exercise, better nutrition, managing stress, seeking DBRU equivalents (i.e., more humor and play), or even by searching for the meaning of life, at least not right away. No, you are more likely to derive unbounded advantages by learning to *want what you have!* As noted, while Miller's work is not primarily about health, it vastly affects it. By learning to want what you have, you will improve your chances to experience beauty, meaning, truth, love, and mystery. If you learn to appreciate these things, then you are more likely, to use Miller's phrase, to succeed in "spitting in instinct's eye." You will be truly blessed—and healthier.

The good/bad news. The good news is that the message sounds simple. It *is* simple, in theory, but the bad news is that it is extremely difficult. Specifically, it's hard to learn and practice thinking in a way that allows you to want what you have. Fortunately, there's more good news: You can improve your chances to do so immeasurably by reading the book, for Timothy Miller seems to be an excellent coach.

The game. Miller perceives the human situation as a playing field, believes the role for his profession (psychotherapy) is to be coaches. The playing field analogy seems apt, as we do compete, our condition is inherently painful, we suffer losses, we have a tendency to break the rules, and we all need coaches at times.

How to play to "win." Learn to want what you have. Be attentive to the present in order that you not undervalue the positive qualities in the moment. Be compassionate, attentive, and grateful! These are the three key principles for overcoming the lust for more.

Compassion, attention, and gratitude. Practicing the qualities of compassion, attention, and gratitude runs contrary to human nature, since wanting more is what comes naturally. To have any chance at wanting what you have and practicing these three qualities, you must be determined, knowledgeable, and resourceful.

Miller describes these concepts in an entertaining and persuasive review of the tenets of evolutionary psychology, with sections on reproductive success in animals and the dynamics of wealth, status, and love. He describes his profession, cognitive therapy, as a discipline that focuses on conscious thoughts and beliefs, habits (often illogical and destructive) and their powerful and inevitable emotional consequences. If submerged and hard to identify, habits can lead to self-defeating behaviors. Coaching can be focused around the daily, lifelong practice of the three principles (compassion, attention, and gratitude) which Miller describes at some length. Fully half the book is devoted to tips, strategies, insights, instruction, and "ten suggestions" for doing so successfully.

As a wellness promoter, I was surprised to discover that I could find so much of interest in a book with subtitles such as "Sorrow, Humiliation, Pain, and Death." Yet, Miller has produced a guidebook for a total way of life built around the three dimensions or principles. No wellness advocate or seeker can afford to ignore these concepts, for they can easily be integrated into all manner of wellness promotion and seeking. (As you can tell, I think *How To Want What You Have* is a terrific wellness book and I recommend it highly.)

NOTES

1. Will Durant, *On the Meaning of Life* (New York: J. J. Little & Ives, 1932), p. 4.

2. Ibid., p. 5.

3. Ibid.

4. Stephen J. Gould, *Wonderful Life* (New York: Norton, 1989), p. 24.

5. Ibid., p. 69.

6. Ibid., p. 54.

7. Ibid., p. 318.

8. Ibid., p. 14.

9. Ibid., p. 15.

10. Ibid., p. 44.

11. Ibid.

12. Ibid.

13. Ibid., p. 48.

14. Ibid., p. 323.

15. James Gleick, *Genius: The Life and Science of Richard Feynman* (New York: Pantheon Books, 1992), p. 12.

16. Ibid., p. 438.

17. David Friend and the editors of *Life* magazine, *The Meaning of Life: Reflections in Words and Pictures on Why We're Here* (Boston: Little, Brown, 1989), p. 7.

18. Irvin Yalom, *Existential Psychotherapy* (New York: Basic Books, 1980), p. 483.

Selected Bibliography

The following is a partial bibliography for books dealing with the meaning of life and a life of meaning. . . . If you know of additional publications that have these two concerns as major themes, please advise. Maybe send a review and, if so disposed, while you're at it, send a commentary on how you find meaning and purpose in life. Merci!

Anderson, W. *Reality Isn't What It Used to Be.* New York: Harper, 1990.
Berman, P. *The Search for Meaning: Americans Talk About What They Believe and Why.* New York:, Ballantine Books, 1990.
Durant, W. *On the Meaning of Life.* New York: J. J. Little & Ives, 1932.
Fabry, J. *The Pursuit of Meaning.* Berkeley, Calif.: Institute of Logotherapy Press, 1968.
———. *Guideposts to Meaning: Discovering What Really Matters.* Oakland, Calif.: New Harbinger Publications, 1988.

Frankl, V. *Man's Search for Meaning*. New York: Pocket, 1963.

———. *The Will to Meaning*. Cleveland: New American Library, 1969.

———. *The Unheard Cry for Meaning*. New York: Touchstone, 1978.

Friedman, D. *Creating Well-Being*. Saratoga, Calif.: R&E Publishers, 1989.

Friend, D., and the editors of *Life* magazine. *The Meaning of Life: Reflections in Words and Pictures on Why We're Here*. New York: Little, Brown, and Time-Life, 1989.

———. *More Reflections on the Meaning of Life*. New York: Little, Brown, and Time-Life, 1991.

Fromm, E. *Escape from Freedom*. New York: Avon Books, 1976.

Gleick, James. *Genius: The Life and Science of Richard Feynman*. New York: Pantheon Books, 1992.

Gould, S. *Wonderful Life*. New York: Norton, 1989.

Harris, F., et. al. *Debates on the Meaning of Life, Evolution and Spiritualism*. Amherst, N.Y.: Prometheus Books, 1992.

Haught, J. A. *Holy Horrors*. Amherst, N.Y.: Prometheus Books, 1990.

Huxley, J. *Religion without Revelation*. New York: Mentor Book, 1957.

Kushner, H. *When All You've Ever Wanted Isn't Enough: The Search for a Life That Matters*. New York: Pocket Books, 1986.

Lamont, C. *The Illusion of Immortality*. New York: Continuum, 1990.

Maslow, A. *The Further Reaches of Human Nature*. New York: Viking, 1971.

May, R. *The Courage to Be*. Toronto: CBC Publishing, 1967.

Miller, T. *How to Want What You Have*. New York: Henry Holt & Co., 1995.

Moorhead, H. *The Meaning of Life*. Chicago: Chicago Review Press, 1988.

Morgan, J. *From Freud to Frankl: Our Modern Search for Personal Meaning*. Bristol, Conn.: Wyndham Hall Press, 1987.

Morley, P. *The Rest of Your Life: Your Personal Plan for Finding Authentic Meaning and Significance*. Nashville: Thomas Nelson Publishers, 1992.

Morris, T. *Making Sense of It All: Pascal and the Meaning of Life*. Grand Rapids, Mich.: Eerdmans Publishing Co., 1992.

Munitz, M. *Does Life Have Meaning?* Amherst, N.Y.: Prometheus Books, 1993.

Myers, D. *The Pursuit of Happiness: Who Is Happy and Why?* New York: William Morrow and Company, 1992.

Nagel, T. *Mortal Questions.* London: Cambridge Press, 1979.

Sanders, S. and D. R. Cheney. *The Meaning of Life.* Englewood Cliffs, N.J.: Prentice-Hall, 1980.

Sartre, J. *Being and Nothingness.* New York: Pocket Books, 1983.

Schopenhauer, A. *The World as Will and Representation.* Indian Hills, Colo.: Falcon's Way Press, 1958.

Tillich, P. *The Courage to Be.* New Haven, Conn.: Yale University Press, 1952.

Ungersma, A. *The Search for Meaning.* Philadelphia: Westminster, 1961.

Watters, W. *Deadly Doctrine.* Amherst, N.Y.: Prometheus Books, 1992.

Watts, A. *The Wisdom of Insecurity.* New York: Vintage Books, 1951.

Wholey, D. *Are You Happy? Some Answers to the Most Important Questions in Your Life.* Boston: Houghton-Mifflin, 1986

Winokur, J. *Zen to Go.* New York: New American Library, 1989.

Yalom, I. *Existential Psychotherapy.* New York: Basic Books, 1980.

About the Author and Contributors*

Judd R. Allen, Ph.D. President of the Human Resources Institute, "Juddski" Allen helps people build cultural environments conducive to personal and organizational well-being. A licensed psychologist, he edits a journal, serves on the faculties of three colleges, and proudly carries forward the pioneering work of his revered father, the late Robert F. Allen. He is an athlete, intellectual, and treasured friend to many, including the author of this work.

---

*This is not a comprehensive list of all the contributors to this work, as some contributors proved unreachable. To those quoted without the benefit of biographical statements who chance to encounter this book, I have a request similar to that addressed to the cute alien in the movie *E.T.*: Contributor, please phone home.

Dale L. Anderson, M.D. Anderson is the author of *Muscle Pain Relief,* which describes an innovative "hold and fold" method of current treatment and future prevention. In the unlikely event that doesn't work (or even if it does!), he also practices a unique brand of humor "for the health of it" called "J'Arm." A practicing physician at Park Nicollet Medical Center in Minneapolis, Dr. Anderson directs the Department of Complementary Medicine, blending "alternative" practices with conventional western approaches.

Donald B. Ardell, Ph.D. The author of *High Level Wellness: An Alternative to Doctors, Drugs, and Disease* and several other books, Donald Ardell publishes the *Ardell Wellness Report* quarterly. He holds degrees from George Washington University, the University of North Carolina at Chapel Hill, Stanford University, and the Union Institute in Ohio. Don has traveled extensively promoting wellness and is a member of the board of trustees of the National Wellness Institute, as well as one of ten recipients of the 1991 American Fitness Leaders Award. He has been a member of the staff of the University of Central Florida since 1985, and is an All-American duathlete and triathlete. In 1994, Don won national and world championships in his division in the sport of duathlon.

Jeanne Louise Ardell. Despite the fact that she is the daughter of the author, Jeanne Ardell's contribution to this book was in no way printed because she addresses her father as "O Well and Witty One, Revered, Admired, and Swooned-Over Worldwide" or, on occasions, as the "Czar of Wellness, Our Paramount Leader, My Emperor of Well-Being."

Virginia Aronson, R.D., M.S. Author of a dozen books (including *The White House Family Cookbook,* coauthored with Chef Henry Haller and published by Random House), in her most recent work, *Different Needs, Different Voices,* Virginia Aronson explores the link between creativity and madness. She also writes plays, poetry, and love-notes to her writer/actor husband.

John Bailiff, Ph.D. Professor emeritus of philosophy at the University of Wisconsin-Stevens Point, where he spent most of his thirty-one-year career teaching philosophy, Dr. Bailiff recently retired to devote full-time to writing, training, and racing. He has been a member of the U.S. Triathlon Team for the past two years, representing his country in world championships in England and New Zealand.

Murray Banks. A former teacher once named Vermont Teacher of the Year as well as winner of the Outstanding Educator Award, Murray Banks conducts over two hundred seminars and motivational keynote speeches on stress, wellness, and performance annually throughout North America. He is a three-time national champion in two sports, triathlon and nordic skiing.

Bob Basso, Ph.D. *People* magazine called Bob Basso "America's Number One Fun-Motivator." A nationally renowned speaker on therapeutic humor, Basso has authored seven books and is a former award-winning news director for NBC and college professor.

Lisa Battaglia, M.S.Ed. The wellness and employee assistance program consultant for the North Carolina League of Municipalities in Raleigh, North Carolina, Lisa Battaglia has more than seventeen years of professional experience in wellness programming. She assists North Carolina towns and cities in designing and enhancing municipal wellness and employee assistance programs.

Jeff Bensky. Known as "Bubbles" to his close friends, Jeff Bensky is a caring individual who helps other people make decisions (what a deal). He is continually searching for the meaning of life through his work.

Francie M. Berg, M.S. Editor of the *Healthy Weight Journal,* Francie Berg adds to her statement on M&P, "Since people, place, and purpose (living for what I believe in) bring meaning into my life, it is my hope for others that they have strong, loving, freeing relationships; live in a place that feels like home; and find a life's work that is challenging, fun, and fulfilling."

Claude E. Berreckman. An attorney in Cozad, New Mexico, Claude Berreckman offered this observation in lieu of personal details: "As (and if) we age, our M&P in life changes drastically. While you can imagine what mine was at seventeen, I am now sixty-one, and my most ardent goal is to create trust funds for the college educations of my three grandchildren."

Barbara Braden. A massage therapist with a psychiatric nursing background, Barbara Braden notes that "Mine is the gift of shared experience of the most intimate kind—that of the mind, body, and spirit—healing is a privilege to witness, a joy to behold."

Celeste L. Budwit. A speaker, consultant, and trainer who lives in Houston with three enlightened cats, Celeste Budwit has her own company (Wellness Unlimited), which focuses on helping firms provide quality health care while containing costs.

Steve Carrell. In ten years of freelance writing full-time from Austin, Texas, Steve Carrell has performed widely varied jobs, including frequent health articles for consumers and health professionals. The subject of M&P prompted him to contribute to this book for free, even though he (1) doesn't like the "free" aspect of freelancing, and (2) believes M&P inextricably involves spiritual issues.

J. Grady Cash. A resident of Hampton, Virginia, when not writing whimsical stories, Grady Cash conducts workshops on values-based money management. He is the author of *Conquer the Seven Deadly Money Mistakes* and director of the Center for Financial Well-Being.

Charles Cochrane (deceased). Having spent his first twenty years in emotional poverty in England, Charles Cochrane emigrated to Perth, Western Australia, via India in 1970. Involved in a series of activities over the years, including outback driller's assistant, teacher of handicapped children, pursuit of a master's degree (exercise physiology), and the America's Cup sailing campaigns, Charles considered himself privileged to live in Oz.

Tom Collingwood, Ph.D. Tom Collingwood holds an M.S. in exercise science and a doctorate in psychology. He has extensive experience in developing fitness programs within law enforcement and the military. An additional focus in his life has been developing and installing fitness programs for substance abuse and delinquency prevention with at-risk youth.

Lisa De Seino. Holding M.S. in counseling and a B.A. in music, Lisa De Seino works with Unity Hospice as a facilitator for grief support groups. She has experience as a music teacher, a coordinator for college students in cooperative education, and a university counselor.

Maureen Dingelstad. A traveller from Aussieland, Maureen Dingelstad seeks experience, understanding, discovery, enjoyment, and warm relationships. To keep travelling—to never arrive—is okay by her, but she hopes for a long journey.

Grant Donovan, Ph.D. A doctoral graduate in performance psychology, Grant Donovan has worked extensively in East Asia, England, and the United States as a corporate coach and sports educator for a wide variety of organizations and teams. Author of six books, Grant edits the *Global Network News,* a publication dedicated solely to work team issues.

Scott Douglas. Editor of *Running Times,* the world's second-largest magazine for runners, Scott Douglas is also the founding editor and publisher of "an underground newsletter" called *Running, Ranting, and Racing.* He holds a master's degree in theology but hasn't been to church in years. Scott prides himself on being that rare adult male whose I.Q. is greater than his weight.

Mary Drabbs. Born and raised in rural Montana, Mary Drabbs taught English for twelve years, then switched gears. After earning a master's degree in physical education, she served as an assistant professor at Eastern Washington University, responsible for directing the campus fitness center. She is currently working toward a Ph.D. in health education at the University of Texas.

Jacque D. Dunegan. Mother of two precious sons, married to the same man for twenty-eight years, Jacque Dunegan is having a great time with life, savoring every moment. She owns a personal training company called Bodygenesis, Inc. and has formed another called Weltrax, Inc. Jacque has a Master's degree in exercise physiology/wellness.

Jay N. Eacker, Ph.D. A professor of psychology at Whitman College in Walla Walla, Washington, Jay is a behavior analyst who has taught seminars and directed undergraduate research on the psychology of health. He also bicycles, skis, plays squash and tennis, and hikes with his wife and family.

Sandra Fedorovich. A licensed professional counselor who works with students at the Mississippi State University Counseling Center, Sandra Fedorovich tries to follow the recommendation of Jonathan Swift: "May you live all the days of your life."

Bob Fellows. Bob Fellows combines a master's of theological studies degree from Harvard University with over twenty years of experience as a professional magician. His "mind magic" captivates audiences worldwide, and motivates them to pursue a wellness lifestyle. Bob is the author of *Easily Fooled* and he currently directs the National Wellness Speakers Bureau.

Tom Ferguson, M.D. Self-care pioneer, health futurist, and founder of the influential journal *Medical Self-Care*, Tom Ferguson is a popular speaker and workshop leader. He lives in Austin, Texas, with his wife, daughter, and their two unpredictable cats.

Carol Filkins, M.S. A resident of Indianapolis, Indiana, Carol Filkins lives with her husband, Derrick, and their cats. She works with the YMCA of Greater Indianapolis and serves as the social coordinator for a close-knit group of friends. Her distinctive laugh will tell you where they are gathered.

Susan B. Frampton, Ph.D. For fifteen years Susan Frampton has worked in hospital and clinic settings managing education and primary health care. She attempts to model (with varying degrees of success) her personal philosophy of "relax, life is short, don't take anything too seriously" both within and beyond the workplace.

Andrea Frank. The founder of the Spiritual Wellness Network, Andrea Frank began the association in 1991 to enhance the learning, sharing, and caring of professionals interested in the relationship between spirituality and health. "Andy" is a community health educator by trade and a member of the Religious Society of Friends (Quakers) by conviction. Her search for the meaning of life continues at the University of Wisconsin-Madison, where she is pursuing doctoral studies in adult education and the history of medicine.

William J. Gaertner, M.D. A family physician in Wisconsin for fifteen years after teaching high school biology and chemistry for eight years, William Gaertner tries to combine what he has learned about taking care of one's health with behavior modification techniques in order to assist his patients to live healthy lifestyles. His special interests in medicine are health promotion and risk factor reduction; in his personal life, his interests are triathlons and tennis.

Carol Garzona. Editor of the *Hope Health Letter,* Carol Garzona lives in Seattle and has "given up on perfecting body and mind." Noting that "none of us gets out of this world alive," she is training instead "to compete in the triathlon of the soul, which means not only seeking out dead bloated rhino underfoot equivalents (DBRUs) but merging into them."

Gerald Gergley, M.S. An associate professor at the University of Central Florida in Orlando, Gerald Gergley is a former wrestler and standout in football, golf, and baseball. He has finished the Hawaii Ironman Triathlon three times and been on the U.S. triathlon team for the last two years (racing in England and New Zealand). An author and popular lecturer, he is a member of the University of Buffalo Sports Hall of Fame.

Izzy Gesell. A public speaker, seminar leader, and writer who believes humor is our most underutilized personal resource, Izzy Gesell's seminars and workshops help individuals and organizations recognize and reap the many benefits of an active sense of humor. Izzy says, "The road to happiness begins with the joy in your heart."

Peter Gianoli. Peter Gianoli is a former health and fitness professional in Western Australia who one day came to a sudden realization that the only way to achieve true wellness was to take responsibility for (and to own) his own business. Seven years later, he does own a business (Charthill Holdings Ltd.), a management and marketing company which busies itself with any project that pays well and sounds exciting.

Joel Goodman. Founder and director of the HUMOR Project in Saratoga Springs, New York, Joel Goodman is described as "the first full-time humor educator in the world." Joel still (occasionally) wonders what he wants to be when he grows up.

Jennifer Heart. Her desirable blood pressure and cholesterol levels, regularly exercised sense of humor, and VO2 (oxygen uptake capacity) max are only surpassed by Jennifer Heart's extraordinarily healthy libido. Maintaining a balanced approach to physical activity, she varies her "horizontal pursuits" with the more orthodox sports, such as running and cycling. Will "sexathons" ever be approved by the International Olympic Committee?

William G. Hettler, M.D. Bill Hettler is a physician, husband, father of six, educator, and amateur athlete. He believes that there is much more that can be done to promote the health of Americans than simply adding more doctors, hospitals, and clinics. Bill is a cofounder of the National Wellness Institute and believes that promoting health is at least as valid an occupation as treating disease.

Steven Jonas, M.D. A professor of preventive medicine at the State University of New York at Stonybrook, Steven Jonas writes about health policy, drug abuse policy, health promotion/disease prevention, and national politics. A triathlete, skier, and devotee of classical music, he loves his family, his life, and being alive.

Deb Jones. Manager of the Workplace Wellness Program for 900 Employees at Vancouver Hospital, Vancouver, British Columbia, Deb Jones is also the director of Well-Advised, a health promotion consulting company specializing in needs assessments, nutrition, and stress management. Deb is a registered dietitian with a master's degree in health promotion. Deb anticipates that her search for M&P will focus in good measure on planning and managing a Canadian Wellness Conference in British Columbia in May 1997.

Peg Jordan. A registered nurse and journalist who edits *American Fitness* magazine, Peg Jordan has authored several books and acts as a health/fitness commentator for Fox Network, CNN, and NBC. She also owns a video and television production company. Peg is a member of the California Governor's Council on Physical Fitness and Sports.

Laurie Kelley. Laurie Kelley resides in Nashville (Music City USA), Tennessee, where she serves as a personal assistant and road manager for Naomi Judd, formerly of the music duet The Judds, now turned best-selling author and speaker. Laurie works with Naomi to spread information about the mind/body connection and its relationship with spirituality and healing. Laurie also speaks and writes about health and wellness, in addition to parenting two cats, Bud and Lilla.

Don Kemper. President of Healthwise, a health promotion firm in Boise, Idaho, Don Kemper has a mountain bike, a cabin in the mountains, and children born in four decades. His lifework is to expand the role of the consumer in medical self-care and medical decision making.

Gloria Kotecki. A wife, mother, nurse, educator, Eucharistic minister, and a Sunday School teacher who enjoys "helping others in any way I can," Gloria Kotecki is a member of the Who's Who Worldwide 1994–1995 Registry of Business Leaders.

Jerry Krause, Ph.D. Jerry Krause serves as fitness and wellness coordinator and professor in the physical education, health, and recreation department at Eastern Washington University in Cheney, Washington. A prolific writer, he's been a physical educator and coach for thirty-five years. Jerry was selected as the Washington Physical Educator of the Year in 1987 and served as a visiting scholar at the U.S. Military Academy in 1992–1993.

John G. Langdon, M.D. Former director of the Student Health Service at the University of Central Florida and coauthor of the book *Wellness: The Body, Mind, and Spirit,* John Langdon is an internal medicine specialist. John is an educator, video personality, researcher, triathlete, sailor, adventurer, skier, and lover, in no particular order.

C. H. "Pete" LeRoy, Jr. "Pete" LeRoy spent a short stint in the armed forces and then completed a degree in physical education at Henderson State University in 1970. A move to Oregon, the passage of a couple decades, a career teaching in public schools, a few master's degrees and a general thirst for knowledge led, eventually, to a doctorate and his current position as head of the health and physical education department at Montana State University-Billings.

Robert H. Lichtenbert. Robert Lichtenbert teaches philosophy at various colleges and universities in the Chicago area. Since January, 1988, Bob has published a sixteen-page quarterly journal entitled *The Meaning of Life.*

Julie T. Lusk, M.Ed., LPC. Director of health management at Lewis-Gale Clinic in Salem, Virginia, Julie Lusk is a former assistant dean of students at Roanoke College and chairperson of the award winning community-based Alive and Well Coalition. She is editor of *30 Scripts for Relaxation, Imagery, and Inner Healing*, volumes 1 and 2. For over fifteen years, Julie has designed and conducted seminars and is a licensed counselor and certified yoga teacher.

Tim Madigan. Executive editor of *Free Inquiry* magazine and coeditor of the *Secular Humanist Bulletin*, Tim Madigan is a doctoral candidate in philosophy at the State University of New York in Buffalo. He travels across the United States and abroad spreading the good word of godlessness. The only spirits he likes are those that follow the strict German Purity Brewing Laws of 1516.

Sandra Martin. Using her twenty years experience in health care, wellness, and organizational health consulting, Sandra Martin conducts seminars and coaches individuals on lifestyle management and personal growth. She has enjoyed and benefitted from her own journey of growth and development and is currently focusing on and researching spiritual well-being.

Jamie Martindale. Vice-president of Health First Consulting Corporation and a creative, enthusiastic, deep-thinker, Jamie Martindale is also a wealthy and famous author trapped in a wellness educator's body. His wife and children can often be found around him at playgrounds and soccer fields.

Susan K. Marshall, M.Ed., M.A. A licensed professional counselor, marriage and family therapist, and yoga instructor, Susan Marshall is wellness educator and president of the Center for Total Wellness in Houston. She believes that everyone has the power to be optimally healthy and happy and, through exploration and integration of body, mind, emotions, and spirit, one's potential can be reached.

Emina McCormack, M.Sc.Ed. Emina McCormack has been director of the University of Vermont Lifetime Wellness Program for over ten years and provides a multitude of wellness programs to faculty, staff, and students. Emina also teaches stress management classes in the Human Development Studies Department. Her personal and professional goals are to find ways to balance home, work, and self as a way of maintaining wellbeing.

Lauve Metcalfe. An expert on lifestyle programs for worksite wellness, Lauve Metcalfe works with many national organizations and corporations to develop and implement employee health, fitness, and behavior change programs. She also conducts workshops for consumer groups on self-esteem, body image, and healthy lifestyles.

Susan Morrow. Susan Morrow is a family therapist in private practice and a trainer/consultant on wellness and human relations issues. She is also the mother of two sons.

Jane E. Myers. A professor of counseling at the University of North Carolina-Greensboro specializing in aging and assessments, Jane's professional positions, research, and writings have focused on the challenges of extending the quality of life for those whom modern science has provided an extended quantity of years.

Gina A. Oliva. A faculty member in the Department of Physical Education at Gallaudet University in Washington, D.C., Gina established "The Gallaudet Workout" and produced the first aerobic video to utilize visual cues. Named a "Healthy American Fitness Leader" in 1989, she travels extensively promoting fitness in the deaf community.

Denise Padilla. Denise Padilla is a graduate student in human resource development and a health promotions coordinator at Colorado State University.

Mike Peterson, Ed.D. An assistant professor at the University of Delaware, Mike Peterson is married and has two daughters. His special interest in meaning and purpose is how these concerns can be related to the work people do, and how pursuing the MOL can benefit an employee's health and QOL (quality of life). When Mike isn't focusing on metaphysical cogitations, he busies himself with something he calls "intraplanetary physical pursuits."

Veronica Pick. Raised in the Pacific Northwest, transplanted to the mid-Atlantic, Veronica Pick is "living every moment of my life, fulfilling all of my dreams, and appreciating the uniqueness of every human being."

Roger J. Plant. Residing in the southwest of Australia, Roger Plant claims eight as a preferred, nominal age, and lives by hope, whimsy, and the dew of small things.

Marcia Poe, R.D.H., M.S. The vice-president of TechniCare Link, a nutritional consulting firm, Marcia Poe also assists "The Tooth Fairy" as a dental hygienist. She teaches nutrition ("the floss for general health") and behavior and clinical ecology.

Rev. Dr. David W. Randle. David Randle is an ordained minister in the United Church of Christ and serves as president of the WHALE (Wellness, Health, and Lifestyle Education) Center. He also holds a doctorate in spiritual disciplines, wellness, and environmental concerns from the University of Northern Colorado. Most of Randle's work consists of training in leadership development and culture change.

Maryann Rapposelli. One of many "thirtysomething" Americans searching for the MOL, Maryann Rapposelli was raised in Delaware and attended the University of Delaware and Eastern Kentucky University in Richmond. Having lived, worked, and played in Kentucky and New York, Maryann is back at the University of Delaware, enjoying a position in the department of recreation.

Rocket Rod Raymond. The director of the life fitness and wellness program at the University of Minnesota-Duluth, Rod states, "I'm just a squirrel trying to get a nut."

Wendy Repovich, Ph.D. Director of the exercise science program at Eastern Washington University in Cheney, Washington, Wendy chairs the department's wellness committee which tries to show by example that it is possible to be healthy and well with very little effort, as long as you are consistent and persistent.

Frank A. Roberts, LCSW. Trained and experienced in healing from the neck up (as a psychotherapist) and from the neck down (as a certified personal trainer), Frank Roberts heads the conditioning program for the Northern Virginia Senior Softball Association. He is grounded by the ideas and traditions that integrate mind and body toward the ultimate in self-actualization.

Karin K. Roberts, R.N., M.N. An assistant professor of nursing for seventeen years at the same college, Karin Roberts finds continuous challenges and new opportunities in her familiar surroundings. "Nothing makes me feel more alive, except my two boys, Keil (age seven) and Nivk (age eleven). They have taught me to see and smell the roses again."

Walt Schafer, Ph.D. A competitive runner for more than forty years and a meditator for nearly half that long, in his spare time Walt Schafer is a professor of sociology at California State University, Chico. In addition to being active in health-related initiatives in his community, Schafer puts to the test his ideas of composure under pressure by kayaking Class IV rivers with his wife and friends.

Neil Schmottlach, Ph.D. The director of the Fischer Institute for Wellness at Ball State University which offers a graduate program in wellness management, Neil Schmottlach coordinates and facilitates wellness activities for the campus community and conducts wellness research and information exchanges nationally. Neil considers his quest for M&P a lifelong journey.

Jenna Scott. Jenna Scott is president of the Donald B. Ardell Fan Club (membership one or more), vice-chair of the Sierra Club of Central Texas, and an owner-handler of show and rescue dogs. She also has a real job trying to steward your tax dollars as a claims representative at the Social Security Administration.

Patti Shank. While managing the health education and training department for a central Maryland H.M.O., Patti Shank's life's work involves questioning, learning, and assisting others towards wherever they're going. Her impudence, humor, and energy have earned accolades from open-minded conference participants—and exasperation from people looking for *the answer.*

Jill Shanks. On a journey of self-discovery while seeking congruency in body/mind and spirit, Jill Shanks is a passionate lifelong learner on a curving path with many peaks and other growth experiences. She is pursuing a doctorate in psychology while directing health promotion for the Midwest Health District in Saskatoon, Saskatchewan, Canada.

Wendy Swain Shore. Wendy Shore is a forty-eight-year-old woman who chooses to have "mother" as her primary occupation. In her spare time, Wendy trains for and occasionally participates in a triathlon. She also loves to dance, travel, and edit the *Ardell Wellness Report.*

Joe Taylor. Editor and publisher of *Active Living,* a newsletter for right-thinking and possibly but not necessarily left-leaning fitness and wellness professionals, Joe Taylor is also author of a book on conditioning for hockey (a sport which is mandatory in Canada) and another on fitness (regarded as subversive by his former peers at the *Toronto Star*). Taylor worked in Zambia for several years and never quite got over it. He is still hopeful elephants will establish themselves in Collingwood, Ontario, where he lives with two dogs, one wife, and a garden.

Linda Tharp, Ed.D. An adjunct faculty member of several Colorado universities in education, psychology, human development, and communication, Linda Tharp has developed an online graduate course on self-care and renewal. Linda facilitates workshops and retreats on these subjects.

Suzanne Tonti. An exercise physiologist by training and a health and wellness promoter by heart, Suzanne Tonti teaches classes and presents workshops on building self-esteem in the workplace, developing a mindset for wellness, and employee empowerment.

Allan Tranter. Director of the Ministry of Sport and Recreation in Perth, Western Australia, Allan Tanter is also a writer; orator extraordinaire; basketball player; lover of red wine, live theater, and eating out; driver of fast cars; traveller to many places; and is aging with dignity.

Jack W. Travis, M.D. In 1972, while completing a residency in preventive medicine at Johns Hopkins University, Jack Travis encountered Halbert L. Dunn's book, *High Level Wellness*. Three years later, while opening the first wellness center in Mill Valley, California, he met Donald B. Ardell. The rest is history. That same year, he created the original *Wellness Inventory* (five hundred thousand copies in print) and since then has coauthored four books, including *The Wellness Workbook*.

William J. "Bud" Wallace. An influential advocate of caning and one of the nation's finest elderly triathletes, Bud Wallace divides his time between Florida's Gulf Coast and New York's seedy inner cities. He has a family but refuses to release any details about his personal life, including educational background, nationality, or race.

James R. Ward. The oldest finisher of the Hawaiian Ironman Triathlon for the past four years, Jim Ward (at seventy-seven years old) has competed (and won his age group) in more than a hundred triathlons since 1986.

Susan Zahalsky, M.D. A specialist in physical medicine and re-habilitation in New York City, Susan Zahalsky emphasizes disease prevention as well as treatment. Water exercise, yoga, and patient self-help groups are incorporated into her practice.